SALES SKILL TRAINING PROGRAM

Boost Your Skills to Become an Effective and Successful Salesperson

MARK DAVIES

UP

URANUS
PUBLISHING

...

ISBN: 978-1-915218-03-2
First Edition: October 2021

websites (Pixabay, Pexel, Freepix, Unsplash, StockSnap, etc.).

Disclaimer Notice:

Please note the information contained within this document is for educational and entertainment purposes only. All effort has been executed to present accurate, up-to-date, reliable, complete information. No warranties of any kind are declared or implied. Readers acknowledge that the author is not engaged in rendering legal, financial, medical or professional advice. The content within this book has been derived from various sources. Please consult a licensed professional before attempting any techniques outlined in this book.

By reading this document, the reader agrees that under no circumstances is the author responsible for any losses, direct or indirect, that are incurred due to the use of the information contained within this document, including, but not limited to, errors, omissions, or inaccuracies.

The trademarks used are without any consent, and the publication of the trademark is without permission or backing by the trademark owner. All trademarks and brands within this book are for clarifying purposes only and are owned by the owners themselves, not affiliated with this document.

TABLE OF CONTENTS

INTRODUCTION

What is selling?

The quick answer is that a sale is a transaction in which a product or service is exchanged for money. The term "selling" may also apply to the practice of persuading someone or someone to buy something.

Of course, the clear answer does not adequately reflect what selling is and looks like in today's world. Selling used to include persuading others (temporarily or permanently) that the good or service you were selling was undervalued at the price you were charging. It was all about ignoring the negative and exaggerating the positive. Selling entailed a series of prominent closing lines and, more often than not, some kind of manipulation.

This was a requirement of being at the top of the business, and it worked because no one had actually implemented their desired protection against these tactics. However, as people became more conscious, those tactics lost their efficacy, and "caveat emptor" reigned once more.

They are still used by carnies, timeshare salespeople, and the odd car salesperson. But, in my opinion, they are wasting their time.

Selling today entails informing the customer and expressing your perspective without making up facts to force the buyer to accept your solution. It involves taking the time to ensure that the buyer and the product are a good match. It's all about understanding the competition's flaws and strengths. It's all about being aware of your own product's flaws and strengths and being forthright about them. It's well-versed in the industry's trends and challenges.

Selling today can be a good experience for both the buyer and the seller if done correctly. Both parties are under less stress. It is more beneficial to all parties.

To summarize, selling is the process of learning about your product, market, and competitors and then exchanging that information to facilitate payments from one party to another in exchange for products or services.

The art of selling is a fascinating topic. It's a complex issue that's been simplified. At its core, selling is about matching expectations and satisfying stereotypes to achieve desired results.

It's important to understand that the distinction between marketing and sale has little to do with what they are in principle and all to do with how you interact with your customer. Marketing focuses on acquiring consumers through advertisement or branding tactics, while a seller's emphasis is on ensuring that there is sufficient availability of goods for them and that customers are aware that they are available.

CHAPTER 1: THE QUALITIES OF SUCCESSFUL SALESPEOPLE

The person who facilitates sales by 'closing the deal' is critical to the organization's success. These individuals are well-trained and experienced in the field of sales. Being intelligent, friendly, and charismatic isn't enough to make someone a "Successful Salesperson." They must also possess the qualities and attributes acquired through extensive research, preparation, and continuous practice. These characteristics or core competencies aid in developing a high level of skill, allowing them to perform better when procuring and closing deals.

A Salesperson's success and results are typically calculated in terms of numbers achieved and revenue produced. The problem with the Sales model is that if salespeople do not meet targets, they are labeled as unsuccessful and denied incentives and benefits associated with their efforts. It contributes to a pessimistic mindset and encourages them to do whatever it takes to close the deal, regardless of the impact on the prospect.

As a result, new sales models and concepts are needed to bridge the gap between the two parties and establish a win-win scenario for both the seller and the potential buyer.

The dynamics of sales are evolving due to the changing economy, developing economies, high competition, and demanding customers. The salesperson in the past was stereotypical, cunning, and unethical, saying anything to close a deal and being self-centered or self-oriented. However, next-generation salespeople are now focused on guiding their prospective customers through the entire sales process by exchanging knowledge, understanding, and details about the goods and services, features and benefits, and what it can and cannot offer, which helps to build confidence. This process is less concerned with selling and more concerned with guiding the prospect through the experience and selecting the product while being fully informed.

The salesperson is introducing improved communication strategies and approaches and a modern approach to transition from old procedures to alternative methods, which is bringing in high-performing salespeople.

These high-performing salespeople are known for their charisma and intellect. They operate so efficiently and effectively that they can open doors to new markets and close sales without difficulty. These salespeople have specific characteristics and discipline that seem to be automatic but are the product of continuous effort, learning, preparation, and practice. Let's look at a salesperson's anatomy, including how they think, perform, and behave.

1. Salesperson's Brain and Mind

The 'brain,' which is made up of nerve cells and blood vessels, has a distinct form. The brain is a vital organ in the human body because it is the nerve system's hub, coordinating activity, emotions, and feelings.

Diseases of the brain can occur, and they can be detected and treated. The 'Mind' has no physical form, cannot be seen or felt, and is not an organ. As part of its work, the mind refers to a person's thought, reasoning, perceiving, feeling, emotions, willingness, and reaction. The mind is a part of the brain that aids in its functions.

Some people believe that the brain and the mind are the same, while others believe they are not. The brain is regarded as a physical entity, whereas the mind is regarded as a mental entity. The brain is in charge of the body's movement and functions, while the mind is in charge of how a person thinks and acts. Both the Brain and the Mind work together to help a salesperson improve their performance:

Uses

Business Acumen: this is useful in two ways. (a) Being aware of and understanding the prospective client's business, as well as identifying the problem areas and support that the client may require; (b) Addressing the right issues and concerns of the prospective client, as well as creating value by solving their problem by providing appropriate products and services as an offering. On the one hand, having Business Acumen makes the salesperson appear smart, intelligent, and knowledgeable. On the other hand, it makes the salesperson appear to be a value creator and problem solver.

Differentiation: This can be categorized into two: (a) separating yourself from your product and services without becoming emotionally attached to them. (b) distinguishing yourself from other competitors who are vying for a small profit in a crowded market. Differentiation helps elevate you to a position where you are recognized as a superior salesperson with strong beliefs and ethics committed to customer-centricity.

Directional Approach: This refers to taking a directional approach during the sales process, which involves (a) setting appropriate targets that are daunting and outside of one's comfort zone; (b) breaking them down into smaller tasks, such as annual, weekly, or regular tasks, or even projects or sections of projects; and (c) completing them one by one and recording progress for analysis. This method will assist you in becoming more coordinated and mindful of your goals and how to accomplish them.

Taking the Right Decisions: Great salespeople gather information from various sources, process it, and make the best decisions possible based on the situation and timing. This allows them to close further sales. Often salesperson must choose between letting go of a sale and not pressuring a customer into purchasing and thinking about the client's viewpoint or letting go of a non-profitable offer.

Know What You're Selling: Successful salespeople prepare by gathering all relevant information and awareness about their company's products and services. In every sales meeting, they are well-presented and informed, and as a result, they close more deals.

2. Salesperson's Eyes

The eyes are the sensory structure of the organs from which we see. They assist in receiving and processing all visuals into stored information, which is then shared with the Brain and Mind. Effective salespeople don't skip even the tiniest detail about their prospects and keep track of it for potential reference, conversation, or use.

Uses

Knowing Who Is Crucial: This is to observe and learn about the potential customer; the individual in front of you and the decision-makers are likely two different people. Knowing who is critical entails getting to know the right person, the decision-maker, bringing him into the conversation, and engaging with him to achieve a successful result and close the deal.

Observe: Salesperson see and observe the prospective client's behavior, personality, taste, desires, needs, requirements, demand, and buying pattern on the one hand, and the issue, discomfort, or disappointment the prospective client may feel or have with the product or services on the other. Good salespeople see it as an advantage on their side and transform it into further business by emphasizing the appropriate problems and solutions.

3. Salesperson's Ears

The ears are a sophisticated and highly sensitive organ. Ears listen to audio, speech, and vibrations and relay them to the brain. Ears also aid in the recognition of verbal messages. The salesperson uses their ears wisely and does not miss even the tiniest nuance of what is being said.

Uses

Listen with full concentration and curiosity: In every sales contact, the salesperson should listen with full concentration and curiosity to establish a stronger connection with the prospect and collect minute information that can be used to close the deal. It's a great way to hear what's being said and learn from it.

4. Salesperson's Nose

The nose is the organ that controls breathing and scent. The nose takes in the fresh air and moves it through specialized cells in the olfactory system, where the brain detects and recognizes smells. This sensory organ is used by a salesperson to detect risk and danger in a situation or atmosphere and to help them.

Uses

Smell your Customer: This does not mean you actually smell your client, but in a sales situation, you can smell the prospective client's intention of purchasing or not buying, interest or no interest, and so on, which can be aided by using sales strategies and tactics to generate interest and attention.

Effective salespeople keep themselves clean and smell decent, which helps them bond more with potential clients during physical meetings.

5. Salesperson's Mouth

The mouth is vital for eating, drinking, and speaking. Our mouth allows us to render various facial gestures when speaking and remaining calm. To make sales interactions more successful and meaningful, salesperson uses their mouths for speaking and facial expressions.

Uses

Storytelling: The art of storytelling is now widely used in sales, and it is a critical component of success. Effective salespeople use this art to create a powerful vision with their words and facial expressions and present to clients how their product and services will benefit them in the future.

The Art of Asking: The best salesperson talks less but enquire more by asking powerful questions that cause the prospect to speak and interact with feelings, allowing them to close more sales.

6. Salesperson's Shoulders

The shoulders are vital because they attach and control the hands and neck. Shoulders may also refer to someone's or something's sense of duty. As the organization's breadwinner, the salesperson bears the following responsibilities.

Uses

Takes Command and Leads: A salesperson can always take the reins and lead by taking control and responsibility of the whole sale, which is a highly motivating endeavor. They are efficient in sales and can be the organization's blue-eyed boy by generating money from sales deals.

7. Salesperson's Heart

The heart is the organ responsible for pumping blood across the body and supplying oxygen, energy, and nutrients to the tissues and cells. Bravery and courage are both synonyms for the heart. Salespeople are recognized for their bravery and courage in the face of adversity.

Uses

Valor and Courage: Obstacles, loss, and rejection are all fears that everybody has. On the other hand, great salespeople are not afraid of these doubts and do not hold back; instead, they overcome all hurdles, challenges, and fears to emerge victoriously. When they are confronted with rejection or defeat, they do not give up; instead, they gather more power, adopt a positive mindset, and devise a strategy to cross the bridge.

The salesperson is a highly motivated, self-driven, and committed individual who is often up for a challenge. They are real achievers, lone wolves, and work ethic killers.

8. Salesperson's lungs

The primary duty of the lungs is to absorb oxygen from the air we breathe and transfer it to the bloodstream and extract carbon dioxide from the bloodstream and expel it when breathing out. This process produces energy, which aids in our movement.

When others are exhausted, the salesperson can still take over, stay inspired, and keep moving forward. They have a good balance of physical and mental energy, which allows them to take on every task and keep going even though others are tired.

9. Salesperson's Spleen

The spleen is the lymphatic system's largest organ, situated under the ribcage and above the stomach on the left side. It acts as a blood filter as part of the immune system, recycling old red blood cells, platelets, and white blood cells and storing them and assisting in the balance of body fluids. The Spleen's job is to alter, purify, and balance the blood and fluid in the body, and the salesperson does the same.

Uses

Self-Learning: A salesperson must adapt to evolving market conditions, update and expand his expertise and skill sets, and strike the best balance between consumer and product offerings to establish a win-win situation for both. They take online and offline classes, subscribe to magazines and newsletters and read books to improve themselves every day.

10. Salesperson's Hands

The hands play an important role in choosing, carrying, gripping, creating, and performing any type of work. It also plays a crucial role in the life of a salesperson by increasing his effectiveness and power.

Uses

Handshake: It is a powerful gesture that, when used correctly, can be very beneficial. When people meet, the first thing they do is shake hands, which is the foundation for a successful relationship.

Hand Movements and Expressions: We use our hands to communicate and describe things during discussions. Hand movement and gestures aid in proper interaction and connection; salespeople often employ these techniques when communicating, resulting in them feeling secure and strong.

11. Salesperson's Legs and Feet

Legs and feet are the lower body parts that are used for walking in and out. The salesperson also uses their legs to determine a client's level of commitment and interest, and they walk in or out of sales if they don't want to close the deal.

Uses

Keep Moving: It refers to progress; legs are signs of progress in life. Effective salespeople keep going forward on their sales path, staying ahead of rivals and closing more and more sales deals, thanks to their experience, skills, and practice.

Know When to Leave: They can recognize when to enter and when to leave any circumstance or sale. They understand that to take a giant leap, they must first take a step back, relax, and then move forward. They are also aware of which of their objectives are practical and which must be abandoned. The effective salesperson can easily assess an opportunity and seize it with their abilities and skills; similarly, some opportunities seem to be a mirage, which they recognize quickly and avoid.

12. Salesperson's Body Language

Body language is a type of nonverbal communication in which physical activity is used to communicate or transmit knowledge. When dealing with potential customers, salespeople use it effectively.

Uses

Body Language Expression: When engaging with potential customers, salespeople use facial expressions, body postures, motions, eye movement, hand movement, touch, and use of space. They used these phrases in their conversations and speeches. The salesperson also mimics and matches their prospective customer's body language to establish a bond and link, contributing to a long-term partnership and sales.

Charisma and Confidence: Self-assurance and charisma are critical aspects of a salesperson's body language because they make them more effective, bold, and effective closers. People like to buy from confident and hardworking people, so developing a positive self-image is important in sales.

13. Other Characteristics of a Salesperson

There are also other things and practices that highly successful salesperson do or follow:

Take Enough Sleep: Everyone needs enough rest to function properly. Successful salespeople are aware of this and ensure that they get enough rest and sleep to stay charged and energized. They also use Tea or Coffee to stay more focused and energized, as some salespeople make it a habit to drink it.

Take Healthy Food and Fluid: A successful salesperson understands the importance of providing healthy food and fluid, and they consume it at the appropriate times. This provides them with the necessary health and energy to keep them going.

Exercise Daily: The salesperson is becoming more self-aware due to shifting patterns. They are including regular exercise in their schedules, which gives them the strength and flexibility to perform more and better physically and mentally.

Honest: With new consumer developments, salespeople are more honest than ever before; they exchange full details with the appropriate viewpoint, and they use various strategies and techniques, such as storytelling and consulting, to increase loyalty and commitment, allowing them to sell more effectively and ethically.

Helpful: Salesperson are shifting their focus from pushing to helping; they communicate with customers more effectively, better understand their problems, and assist them in selecting the best products and services to meet their needs.

Use Organizational Software: Today's businesses spend a lot of money on various tools and apps to help salespeople be more efficient. Salesperson effectively utilizes these technologies and software, resulting in increased efficiency and more time to prepare and execute better.

Maximize CRM: Salesperson is no longer cold calling because the efficacy of the cold calling is poor, and the outcomes are unpredictable. As a result, salespeople are communicating more with their customers and providing after-sales services, which aids in the development of stronger customer relationships and the generation of positive referrals. "A satisfied customer refers to another satisfied customer," as the old sales adage goes. Salespeople who are highly effective and successful are constantly working to improve their CRM.

Scheduling: Because productive and efficient salespeople understand that time is money, they arrange or organize their meetings and appointments as part of their daily routine and record it in their planner or scheduler.

Above are the characteristics of a Salesperson. Suppose you want to be a highly efficient and productive salesperson. In that case, you must learn these and put them into practice right away in each sales meeting or any meeting or conversation, official or personal, and you will see a significant difference in the way you interact, with a very positive outcome.

CHAPTER 2: TYPES OF SALESPERSON

Salespersons are professional individuals who perform direct selling for a company, which may involve face-to-face or telephonic sales affected by direct or indirect sales. They assist consumers in making purchasing decisions by seeking or motivating them to do so.

Seller-initiated efforts are those that salespeople initiate to convert potential buyers into buyers. With various types of prospective customers, salespeople act, respond and communicate in different ways. Since each customer is unique, the salesperson must have extensive knowledge of the product and services, competitors and their products, and understand the client's needs and requirements.

We define sales as the art of persuading people to purchase what a salesperson has to sell. Everyone uses the art of persuasion and influencing at some point in their lives, so we can assume that everyone is a salesperson in their own right. Improving these skills is a brilliant idea.

A salesperson's job is to make deliberate attempts and follow-ups to persuade a potential customer to buy something he hasn't yet purchased. To put it another way, salespeople assist buyers in removing any doubt, mistrust, apprehension, concern, ignorance, or emotional objections they might have about purchasing or choosing to purchase. Salespeople work hard to gain the confidence of their customers, which leads to sales and satisfaction.

As we all know, each individual is unique, and the Salesperson is no exception. Many characteristics distinguish Salesperson, including their personality, knowledge, experience, skills, interests, choices, style, opinions, initiatives, how they behave, respond, or communicate, interpret things, decision-making abilities, learning abilities, etc. There are four broad categories of salespeople mentioned below.

The Four Types of Salesperson can be summarized as follows:

1. Highly Effective Salespersons: Those who close the most sales are known as Highly Effective Salespersons. During the sales process, these Salespeople are laser-focused on preparation, strategizing, and execution. They are well-prepared, empathetic, resilient, truthful, persistent, positive, concentrated, and business-oriented, and they have all of the necessary knowledge, skills, experience, and expertise. They are imaginative, inventive, and pioneering in their behavior, and they excel at establishing relationships with their clients. These Salespersons are considered all-rounders and are still in high demand.

2. Problem Solver Salesperson: These salespeople excel at prospecting, strategizing, and assessing, but they struggle with closing. They are excellent at generating leads and nurturing them to the next stage, but when it comes to closing, they often exaggerate the conversation and may not result in a sale being closed. They are also knowledgeable and experienced, as well as excellent communicators.

3. Problem Seeker Salesperson: This kind of salesperson isn't very good at planning, strategizing, or prospecting. They are extremely hard workers who work without guidance or a predetermined schedule. They still fail and fall short when it comes to closing sales. They still blame something or someone else for their shortcomings, such as timings, customer demands, product flaws, bad weather, or resource problems, and blame circumstances or others.

4. Salesperson who builds relationships with clients: These salespeople depend on communicating with clients, gaining their confidence and rapport, and developing relationships. They are excellent at developing relationships but not so much at prospecting and converting leads into sales. It is often discovered that they spend most of their time establishing relationships rather than concentrating on sales closure. They concentrate on client management, but they fall short when it comes to prospecting and opportunity conversion.

Every salesperson is different and has different qualities; but, if they strive to develop their skills by refining, studying, and practicing, they can become Highly Effective Salesperson who can close the majority of sales calls, achieve their budgets or deadlines, and benefit for themselves and the company.

Habits of a Highly Effective Salesperson

A habit is a fixed pattern or routine of conduct that is practiced automatically and without being aware of it. Habits are formed by repeating a certain way of thinking, feeling, or acting. People with good habits are praised and admired, and good habits are often beneficial to achieving life success. With continuous practice and deliberate effort, people can shape, influence, and change their habits.

Habits aid in improving a person's productivity. The brain creates patterns by repeating acts and behaviors regularly. When we form habits, repetitive tasks become automatic, and we don't have to exert any effort to complete them. Something that is performed for the first time appears complicated, but it becomes easier and easier when you repeat it. In such activities, this saves mental strength, time, and resources.

Salesperson are aware of the fact that they must constantly strive to improve their positive behaviors. They understand that the influence of habit will help them make meaningful changes in their lives. They keep a close eye on their patterns and take corrective steps to change or correct them to be successful:

Self-Check and Self-Analysis: Salespeople are often aware of their positive and negative behaviors, and they track them and correct them as needed.

Salespeople constantly strive to improve themselves to develop healthier habits and behaviors that will help them achieve success in all aspects of their lives. The Great Habits of Highly Effective and Successful Salesperson are mentioned below.

- *An Inquisitive Learner*

People who have completed their General Education or Management Studies try their luck with various career openings but cannot find anything they like and enter the sales force. Any other salesperson you encounter has a similar story. They have no prior sales experience or expertise. Sales training may or may not be provided by their employers. Over time, they learn sales and begin to produce numbers, and as their knowledge grows, so do their sales skills. The difference between a decent salesperson and a great salesperson is his ability to learn and improve every day.

How to become a curious learner

Do what you are passionate about. The reason for this is simple: when you are passionate about something, you want to develop your skills and enjoy finding new ways to do so. Salesperson who is enthusiastic about their jobs and is lifelong learners have an insatiable appetite for learning new ways to expand their knowledge and experience, and they make time to hone their skills. They enjoy self-improvement and learning new things. To stay effective and lifelong learners, salesperson do the following, which you can try as well:

Find A Mentor: Getting a mentor is the most difficult of all the tasks. Look for it. Approach anyone who is already effective in your field of expertise and ask them to mentor you. Having the right mentor will save you years of hardship and hard work. These individuals have a wealth of knowledge and wisdom, and they can serve as excellent advisors and mentors. To learn from these mentors, develop your listening skills, and become a stronger mentee.

Hire a Coach: Many coaches are available today, all of whom are experts in their fields; however, you must be specific about what you want from them. There are expert coaches in various fields, including leadership, target setting, sales ability, attitude, etc. For effective results, you need to know what area you want to focus on, talk to the coach about it, and have a clear plan.

Read Books: Books are everyone's best friends, and they have a lot to offer in terms of intelligence, experience, abilities, and expertise. Books are one of the most effective ways to learn and store information for future use. Reading and taking notes are the best ways to learn, and implementing them in your life, no matter how small, will have a huge effect over time. Good people are said to be voracious readers. "Readers of Today, Leaders of Tomorrow," as the saying goes.

Participate in some online or in-person training programs: You can enroll in either short-term or long-term courses to improve your knowledge and expertise. There are many ways to improve your knowledge and skills by enrolling in one of the many courses available.

Become a member of or form a mastermind group: It will be a fantastic opportunity to join or form a community of people who are eager to learn and develop. It will aid in peer learning by allowing them to share ideas and best practices and motivating them to learn new things and share in groups.

- **Dress to Impress**

Salesperson are known for their appearance, clothing, attitude, presentability, confidence, and charisma. As a result, salespeople pay close attention to their appearance. Every company adopts a dress code for their employees, especially those in sales and customer service.

The First Impression: When interacting with a new individual, you have seven seconds to make a good first impression. Salespeople are often dressed to make an excellent first impression and are well-dressed for their sales meetings.

Body Language and Tonality: Salesperson's body language and tone play an essential role in their performance. Throughout the meeting and debate, they have clear body language and flawless speech.

No to Tobacco and Cigarettes: If a salesperson has a tobacco or cigarette habit, they can give it up before a meeting and take a mint instead.

- **Domain Expert**

The term Domain Expert or Subject Matter Expert is synonymous with a salesperson. Experts are professionals with a high degree of experience in their field who understand their clients' needs and requirements and have the best possible solution. Some seasoned salespeople exude confidence, loyalty, and integrity.

The salesperson with a higher degree of domain knowledge has a deeper understanding of a particular vertical or sector and engage in constructive conversations with potential customers, which helps create confidence and makes it easier to get to know the customer, which aids in closing. This is a habit that highly successful salesperson build, and you can learn it by doing the following:

Build Expertise Knowledge: Working in a specific area and receiving training in that field or topic aids in the development of expertise knowledge. Knowledgeable salespeople are regarded as trusted advisors and consultants, and they add more value to their clients' lives.

Better Understand and Analyze Clients: Domain expert salesperson has the knowledge and experience to better understand and analyze their clients' needs and requirements and provide appropriate solutions.

Develop a Relationship: A domain specialist salesperson who has Rapport loves authoritative content. Clients regard them as equal to their competitors, if not superior, and are treated with respect and importance. This aids in the development of relationships and the acquisition of revenue.

- **Enthusiasm**

Enthusiasm is described as the eagerness and enjoyment with which people engage in a particular activity. People are drawn to a salesperson because of their energy and excitement, and they become engrossed in what they have to sell.

Highly successful salespeople are often prepared for any sales meeting, inbound or outbound, and bring their attitude, energy, and excitement with them, all of which contribute to their success. Their excitement is infectious, and it transfers to their prospect, connecting their emotions and feelings, which aids in forming a connection. More passion and enthusiasm contribute to more sales.

A highly successful salesperson understands that excitement and enthusiasm can be conveyed in various ways, including speech, body language, and facial expressions. They use all of them to their advantage to convert more sales. This is a habit that highly successful salesperson build, and you can learn it by doing the following:

Being Curious: Curiosity is the salesperson's guiding power, leading to a desire for more. They want to increase their business, convert new leads, and pursue larger deals. Curiosity is a critical element in generating enthusiasm.

Engagement Follows Interest: Salesperson maintains their curiosity and remains active at all times, which allows them to be more efficient and produce more results.

Seeking Knowledge: Discovering new information is always thrilling. The salesperson understands the value of experience and works hard to acquire more. Salespeople understand that the more they practice, the more excited they will become, which will open up more doors and provide insight into potential customers.

The salesperson who believes in themselves stands out because they are conscious of what they are saying and doing with complete trust, confidence, and self-belief.

Highly successful salespeople understand that a motivating speech or instruction is just for a short period and that true inspiration comes from inside. Therefore, these people are always looking for inspiration from inside and pursuing reasons to be inspired and enthusiastic.

Having a Clear Goal: Salesperson have a clear goal in mind, whether to make money, advance in their careers, gain new skills, travel, or create value for themselves and others. They are always enthused about achieving their goals, which motivates them to keep moving and rising.

Be a better team player: Energetic salespeople are always in demand, and any team leader will gladly accept them into their ranks. They are excellent motivators and supporters of their peers and schools, and they are always valuable team players.

- **Customer First**

In the business world, "Client is King" or "Client is God." Every salesperson must handle their customers in the same way, prioritizing their needs and requirements. The salesperson must aspire to develop sound and positive relationships with their customers and add value and knowledge to their lives to gain more business.

Salesperson always thank their customers for their time and business, and they ask for input from time to time to improve. They are constantly looking for new ways to communicate with their customers and consider their needs and desires and what they will need in the future. They share this information with their companies, which aids in developing new products and services and the addition of new features to existing products and services, with the overall aim of better serving customers.

- **An Empathetic Listener**

Highly successful salespeople are often empathetic, compassionate, and understanding as they listen to what matters to their customers and allow them to share their thoughts and concerns. They try to consider their perspective without being judgmental, which helps them interact with customers more and close more deals. When their customers talk, they are always cautious; they listen carefully, consider their needs and requirements, and listen to their anger and dissatisfaction. The viewpoints of clients are more important than their own.

- **Efficient Communicator**

Since sales are all about contact, the salesperson must be effective communicators. This involves both written and verbal communication, and both should be effective and straightforward about what they're trying to say. They interact well with the audience and adapt to the circumstance and requirements. Their language should be straightforward, direct, and easy to comprehend. When communicating with a customer, a highly successful salesperson maintains patience. They control themselves and the situation well when customers are in a bad mood, upset, and shouting. They react appropriately if anything goes wrong. Effective communication can result to:

Feedback and Follow-Up: The salesperson takes real customer feedback and shares it with management to take effective action. They still maintain contact with their customers and follow up on any updates, purchases, and after-sales programs, as well as ensuring proper closure.

Referrals: Successful salespeople keep their customers happy and maintain a positive relationship with them. These customers are a great source for good referrals, and salespeople know that the conversion rate from these referrals would be much higher than any other method of prospecting and calling. As a result, they ask their clients for references and follow up on them.

These are the practices of a highly successful salesperson, and they obey them with such grace that it seems to be second nature to them. Slowly and steadily, with regular and consistent practice, one can develop these habits and be confident that they will yield incredible results and success far beyond one's wildest dreams.

CHAPTER 3: MASTERING THE 'ART OF SELLING'

"Everybody makes a living selling something."
- Robert Louis Stevenson

Robert Louis Stevenson's quote could not be more accurate. It perfectly encapsulates the path of life. Hardcore sale is the beginning and the end of Life. If you believe it or not, selling is the first ability a child learns; he knows from the moment he is born that his cute smile and scrunchy face will win him cuddles and chocolates from the elders. And if he's with a bunch of babies, maybe a bawl would suffice. Within the first few months, math, sales strategies, and skills are mastered, and they are then polished throughout life.

These abilities are then put to use at work, where they are essential. You not only sell yourself (your brand) at work but also the company you work for and its products. So, everything you've gotten so far in life, and everything you'll get in the future, is a result of selling something - your talents, abilities, organization's brand, or goods.

This begs the question: **why are sales so important, and why is it necessary for everyone to sell?**

1. **That is the only way to let the world know what you have to give** - A quiet but highly skilled individual will go unnoticed, while someone who can speak and articulate his abilities (even if they are limited) can catch his target's attention and close the deal.

2. **It helps build relationships** – Yes, sales can and do help build personal and professional relationships when handled properly and without being too pushy. It's the most efficient way to share your story with the rest of the world and communicate with others.

3. **It aids in the development of reputation** – Sales is, to some degree, all about engagement and execution. When you commit and follow through, you build a reputation, which leads to more business, connections, and friends.

These three factors are the foundations of individual and organizational performance. When properly used, they will lead you from one success to the next or put it another way, from one good sale to the next. No one, absolutely no one, will get by without selling, regardless of their place in the company's hierarchy, at home, or in society.

If you hold something of value, you must sell it. You must also sell if you want to know what what you have is worth selling. It's the ultimate feedback tool for your personal brand and everything else you're associated with, in a way.

Now, if it is such an essential life skill and the first that anyone learns, why is it that only a few people - the leaders - are excellent at it, and their talents, services, and goods are in high demand without them having to sell?

What characteristics do leaders have that allow them to be master sellers?

1. **Self-Assurance** – They are confident in their ability/product, understand its worth, and are proud to be associated with it.

2. **Dedication** - Leaders are dedicated to achieving their vision, task, or objective. They go for it with passion, taking no shortcuts.

3. **Integrity** – Leaders must have a solid moral compass and be frank with all stakeholders, including the company, staff, suppliers, and consumers.

4. **Superior soft skills** – Leaders understand how to handle others, whether they be business colleagues, partners, or clients. They treat others with courtesy and respect. Good

leaders prioritize establishing a partnership before closing a deal.

5. Lifelong learners – Leaders constantly update their experience and skillset, which they freely share with their team. Not only that, but they also solicit feedback and, if it is accurate, they act on it.

6. Goal-oriented – Leaders are goal-oriented; they organize and execute according to the plan.

7. Excellent listeners – They are excellent listeners. They pick up on subtle clues and tell when a deal can be explored further or when they need to back off without clear communication.

8. Effective communicators – In addition to being good listeners, leaders are skilled at making small talk. The 'you attitude' is an important way for a leader to put people at ease and get them to listen to what he has to say.

9. Problem solvers – Leaders are problem solvers by nature. Rather than allowing a problem to fester, they address it as soon as possible.

10. Product and business awareness – last but not least, they have in-depth product knowledge and are aware of how the market in which they work works and where it is going – in other words, they are not only concerned with the current but also with the future.

This will lead some of us to wonder: if I have all of the qualities mentioned above, at least to some degree, why am I not considered a leader? What's the difference between the two?

• All of the qualities mentioned above are thoroughly cultivated in a leader;

• It is not only the qualities but also how they use the techniques that make all the difference.

So, in addition to these characteristics, a leader employs some sales techniques that distinguish him from the competition.

What exactly are these techniques?

Transaction-based sales, relationship-based selling, diagnostic selling, and conviction-based selling are the four forms of selling. The first three forms of sale are based on data followed by specific tools and strategies, personal relationships based on confidence (subtle emotional manipulation), or time. We strive to 'push' the commodity into the market by using all of these variables to our benefit, which often results in a forced sale. Both of these are avoided by leaders.

Instead, they use the conviction-based selling strategy, fueled by their enthusiasm for their field of knowledge and the environment surrounding it. This generates a 'pull' impact, or 'attraction,' towards the leader, resulting in a demand for his knowledge, skills, services, and goods.

The following is an easy way to describe this. For example, there are several high-rise buildings in Dubai, but when asked to name them, only one name comes to mind: Burj Khalifa. What is the reason for this? Since it is the tallest and most recognizable. The same is true of leaders; we only remember the best of them – those who know how to put their strengths to good use.

Sales Methodologies and Tools

Salespeople have a difficult time following the sales process. Highly Effective Salesperson don't like it either, but they stick to it faithfully and diligently. The sales method is a step-by-step guide to what needs to be accomplished and how it should be done, while tools help us track, analyze, and improve performance at each step.

The sales process aids in deeper understanding at all levels, as well as the development of sales and marketing strategies. It also aids in moving prospects into the purchasing process more rapidly and smoothly, resulting in the creation and maintenance of long-term consumer relationships. It contributes to adding value to consumers' lives, lowering consumer acquisition costs, increasing quality referrals, and increasing revenues.

The sales process allows a salesperson to be in full charge, removing the possibility of being overwhelmed by emotion, distraction, or something else. Self-regulation, which involves self-control or discipline, adaptability, trustworthiness, honesty, and creativity, is essential for maintaining control. Such salespeople have more leverage over any usual or difficult situation and can use it to their advantage.

A successful salesperson does the following:

Customer Relationship Management (CRM) refers to the management of customer relationships. CRM is a system-based application that records client calls, disruptions, profiles, needs, specifications, and other client-related details, as well as the date of the call or meeting and possible calls or meetings. This allows you to keep track of any conversation and can be a very useful method for recognizing consumer profiles, evaluating them, and using them for more effective communication, contributing to higher conversion. This program is also helpful in prospecting or generating referrals, and it is updated regularly.

Sales process and software assist salespeople in checking, measuring, controlling, and optimizing their results. It becomes automated when they use it daily, and they profit from following the procedure.

Time Management: Following the sales process to the letter helps develop the successful practice of time management, which is one of these highly productive salesperson's main strengths. They plan ahead of time for each operation, divide their time between tasks methodically and productively, and still assist others in achieving better outcomes.

Uses

Help In Remembering Things: Since the human mind is restricted in its ability to retain knowledge for a limited period, a highly successful salesperson will still own the correct information or any commitments made, and they remember all that they have recorded well and can use this information for future contact, reference, business prospecting, or fulfilling their promises by using these resources.

Leaders use these tactics to build a need for what they have to give, explain how to use it, convey its availability, and consistently deliver a high-quality service or product to gain reputation, which contributes to word-of-mouth marketing and eventually consumer demand. There will be no overt sale.

Leaders recognize the value of word-of-mouth referrals focused on long-term, reliable, and high-quality results. They focus on delivering high-quality results and leave the sale to the customers. Consumers sell their satisfaction from associating with an individual and their satisfaction from using a service or product to others, who then 'demand' the person's time/skill, service, or product based on this feedback.

This is how successful leaders sell-by persuading people to buy rather than selling!

CHAPTER 4: SELLING ETIQUETTE

In simple terms, etiquettes refer to a person's personal and social good manners or behavior. Etiquette refers to the rules that govern a person's socially responsible actions.

Salespeople adhere to etiquettes as a part of their personality because it makes them seem more cultured and allows them to talk and act in a polished manner, impressing potential customers, coworkers, bosses, subordinates, and superiors. The salesperson uses proper etiquette in their conversations and is willing to assist them in their professional and personal lives. It aids them in gaining recognition, admiration, and confidence, as well as building loyalty.

In today's intensely competitive market world, sales etiquette is crucial. "People do business with people they like," as the saying goes. Clients would do business with the salesperson they want and who they know they can depend on and trust. That is only possible through fair business practices and proper sales etiquette. Sale is a high-pressure task with quarterly or monthly goals and budgets to meet. The salesperson must contact their customers to meet these targets, and in some of these high-pressure times, they lose their etiquettes and rush to meet their targets. They take a short-term approach in these acute cases, and they lose their current best clients as well as potential clients.

Highly Effective Salespersons, on the other hand, do not abandon their etiquettes and principles under any serious or adverse circumstances; instead, they take a long-term approach and act accordingly, always putting their clients first. This approach helps them gain confidence and loyalty from their clients, and it allows them to always be at the top of any game.

To be a Highly Effective and Successful Salesperson, you must have a genuine concern for your clients and adhere to the highest standards of business etiquette in the sales conversation. Clients' perceptions of you as a professional can influence whether they want to do business with you. As a result, etiquettes can be described as a code of conduct and actions that the Salesperson always observes and obey in all corporate, professional, and personal relationships. That is what makes them so good in every way.

Highly Effective Salesperson follows the following Business or Sales Etiquettes:

• **Be Prepared**: Successful salespeople are always ready and well-prepared. They have the necessary skill sets and knowledge of the products and services they provide. They are often aware of their client's requirements and desires, as well as his personality and behavior. The salesperson is still prepared to deal with his clients' objections or disconnects, if any.

• **Greet First**: To be competitive and make a good first impression, salesperson always greets their clients first and use appropriate greeting terms.

• **Pay Attention To Names**: A person's name is the most significant aspect of their identity since it is how others remember them. You pronounce the name correctly; if you are unsure, you can ask them how to pronounce it correctly. If you're having trouble remembering names, break them down into bits and memorize them. Use them three or four times throughout the conversation.

• **Introduce Yourself in a Polite and Clear Manner:** As a Salesperson, you must introduce yourself politely and clearly if you meet with a client or arrange a meeting with their representative. State your full name, the company you represent, and how you can build or add value to the prospective customer, or what solution you can offer to their need.

• **Obtain Permission:** If you're meeting a client without an appointment, ask for permission by saying, "Is it a good time to talk?" or "Can I speak with you for a moment?" Whenever you propose something during the conversation, ask for permission and say things like, "May I offer some alternatives, if they are suitable for your situation," etc.

• **Always be respectful:** Always try to be respectful during important communications and use phrases or words like "excuse me," "thank you," "please," "you are welcome," and so on. You must always express gratitude to others for providing you with the opportunity to meet or do business with them. Always welcome newcomers to the community or meeting and clarify their position as well as the discussion agenda. Hand over the card with both hands, a card facing the other person, and take their card with both hands, reading the card before putting it in your diary or pocket.

• **Always Be Courteous to Everyone You Meet:** You must always be courteous to everyone you meet and treat them with dignity and respect. It aids in gaining the trust and confidence of everyone you come into contact with.

• **Attend All Meetings On Time:** If you have taken time from a client, you must arrive on time and ensure that you know the client's time.

• **Switch off Your Phone or put on Airplane Mode:** Remove all distractions, particularly your cell phone, before entering a meeting or conversation with a client. Either switch your phone off or set it to Airplane Mode.

• **Don't Just Listen, Pay Attention:** Salesperson pays close attention to what others are saying and looks for further points to move the conversation forward and lead it in his direction by interjecting at the appropriate moment and asking the right question or making suggestions. The majority of the time, the Salesperson behaves as a Listener rather than a Speaker during the entire conversation. Throughout the conversation, the Salesperson uses phrases such as "I understand," "How Interesting," "really," "this is great to know or hear," "nice to know this," "thanks for sharing," "that's awesome/wonderful," and so on.

• **Display the Appropriate Emotion at the Appropriate Time:** During a face-to-face meeting or on the phone, a salesperson may change a client's perception of the company and the salesperson. As a result, scripting can assist in knowing and selecting the appropriate words and using them appropriately to generate the desired effect. Using the appropriate emotion during a conversation will add spice to it. a) Enthusiasm when introducing oneself and the organization; b) Curiosity when building interest and trust between the Salesperson and the Client; c) Encouragement to gain more information, support, and cooperation from the client; d) Calm when disarming and diffusing a situation; e)

49

courteous throughout the discussion. To gain more control over the situation and get the most out of it, use these feelings interchangeably.

• **Don't Hide, Be Honest:** Salesperson must share all necessary details with customers, and they should never hide anything. Instead, they should always be honest and share all relevant information about their products and services. They demonstrate the appropriate value for the product or service proposition as well as the value they bear. It aids in the development of confidence and contributes to increased sales.

• **Remain Focused and Controlled:** Clients may often act in such a way that you're unsure if they're interested or not. In such a situation, you must remain concentrated and in command of the situation and obey any secret signs or messages to get the conversation back on track.

• **Always be adaptable:** You must be adaptable enough to deal with the situation and make necessary adjustments. You should approach your client with an open mind and change your tone, speech, and pace to match theirs. Find a point of correlation and make use of it.

• **React Quickly:** When a client has a question, doubt, or concern, it must be addressed as soon as possible to satisfy the client. Often, check to see if you've solved the issue completely and to the client's satisfaction.

• **Don't Over-commit:** Salesperson must be rational in their projections and honest with their details, and they must not over-commit or make promises they can't keep. Since this may result in a negative opinion of the Salesperson and the company. As a result, before making a commitment or making promises, the salesperson must be assured in all aspects.

• **Positive Body Language:** Throughout the interaction, the salesperson must maintain positive body language. From greeting and handing over the Visiting Card to presenting oneself and closing the deal.

Etiquettes are often beneficial in establishing an immediate and more substantial connection with anyone you encounter, contributing to various benefits.

Benefits of Etiquettes

• **Personal safety:** You will feel more at ease if you know how to act properly in a situation.

• **Protect other people's feelings:** When you use Etiquette, you make others feel at ease and project their emotions. You should not point out other people's faults, show their shortcomings, or call attention to their errors.

• **Encourages Open Communication:** Etiquette encourages people to connect by breaking down barriers. It causes the other person to react more positively, increasing the likelihood of successful communication.

• **Make a Good First Impression:** The first seven seconds of meeting someone are critical, and practicing proper etiquette will help you make a good first impression. An excellent first impression sticks with an individual for a long time.

• **Increase Your Trust and Self-Esteem:** When you use etiquettes properly, you will increase your confidence when meeting new people. You don't have to be concerned with what you're doing or saying when talking with them. It immediately goes appropriately and ideally, if you observe it daily. This leads to increased self-assurance and self-esteem.

• **Develop Strong Relationships:** Etiquette aids in making people feel at ease in our presence and treating them with compassion, courtesy, and respect. This increases our likeability and trustworthiness, resulting in better and stronger relationships.

• **Increases Happiness and Satisfaction:** Being kind and using etiquettes increases happiness and satisfaction.

• **Increases Opportunities:** As opposed to their peers and rivals, people who adopt proper etiquette in all business conditions have a higher chance of gaining new opportunities.

• **Organizational Efficiency:** When etiquettes are part of an organization's culture, they raise morale and foster positive relationships with all stakeholders, including clients. As a result, the organization's overall productivity improves. The boost in morale aids the company in increasing productivity, efficiency, quantity, and customer retention, all of which contribute to overall business development.

Etiquettes assist in displaying appreciation and consideration for others, as well as making them feel comfortable. Etiquette rules can differ or change depending on the place, culture, and personal preferences. In sales and business meetings, you must also observe proper etiquette. It aids in developing customer confidence and rapport, resulting in improved relationships that aid in closing sales.

CHAPTER 5: UNDERSTANDING BUYERS: TYPES OF BUYERS

Advertisements, coupons, discounts, deals, and celebrities are all used by businesses to attract or lure customers. However, these steps affect the Client's decision to some degree, but the Buyer considers other elements when purchasing.

Buyers' behavior determines their purchasing choices, and several factors draw or repel them. The Buyer's behavior is influenced by personality traits, needs, interests, likes, dislikes, experiences, behaviors, and established trends, all of which affect the Buyer's decision-making when making a purchase. In certain situations, buyers follow the same trends and processes; observing and studying these patterns will help you understand how to handle them and deliver your goods and services to get better results.

As a result, identifying and separating the different types of buyers is critical for both the salesperson and the company. You will have the best choices to appeal to your Buyer's needs because you know what kind of Buyer they are. Often, since each person is unique, they have different thought processes, attitudes, behaviors, and mindsets.

Based on the above factors, there are a few explanations that assist the Buyer in thinking in a certain way and making a purchasing decision. These are the factors:

Likes and Dislikes: One of the most significant factors is that buyers have preferences for certain goods, services, or brands. They choose whether or not to purchase the product based on their preferences. iPhone owners, for example, are unlikely to turn to another brand.

Based on the requirements: Another aspect that influences the purchase of goods and services is the Buyer's needs and requirements. In some instances, a buyer decides to purchase a product or service because they desire it. Other times, the buyer does not have to purchase the products or services but does. This may be due to a better offer or contract or the product's anticipated scarcity. For example, when the

Corona Virus breaks out, the cost of masks and sanitizers skyrockets.

Another critical aspect buyers consider when choosing particular products, services, or a brand is experience. For example, if a Buyer has already had positive interactions and moments with the brand's products or services, they will continue to do so until they have a negative experience. Usability, ease of use, the onboarding procedure, or the service and support provided by company representatives may all be factors.

Price: It plays an important role in buyer's purchasing decisions because there are two groups of buyers: a) those who seek out inexpensive alternatives or discounted goods and services, and b) those who seek out expensive and high-quality products, regardless of price.

Brand features and style are also critical factors buyers consider when choosing or purchasing products. Buying a car, for example, necessitates extensive research into the features and appearance of the vehicle.

Compatibility: Since the world is evolving quickly and we see new technological advancements daily, the products and services a Buyer is considering must be equivalent to the changing environment and technological advancements. Cell phones, for example, are continually improving their technology, and the phone we're using is still updating its operating system regularly.

Companies deliver better goods and services than their rivals, which is one of the most significant factors these days. They can accomplish this by regularly updating your goods, facilities, and technology and providing more choices than the competition. For instance, all banks are concentrating on improving their products and services for their customers.

Ease of Use: The product or service that a Buyer is buying should be simple and straightforward to use. Since the world is moving so quickly and everyone is complaining about such a short period, everyone needs goods and services that are simple to use and run. Online banking and mobile banking, for example.

Emotional Connection: This is another significant aspect that influences the Buyer's buying decision. Buyers are motivated to buy goods or services when they connect their feelings and emotions with the product or service, the brand, or the company's representatives, and vice versa.

These are a couple of the most important things buyers consider when making a buying decision. These considerations apply to all Buyers and aid in determining the value of products and services before making a purchase decision. Now we'll go over the different types of buyers in more detail.

Buyers can be divided into five broad groups, as shown below:

To know how they act when making a purchasing decision, the Seller company or Salesperson must consider the prospective buyer's buying habits. Some Buyers make snap decisions, while others take their time; some are loyal to brands, goods, and services, while others choose the best price or option; some Buyers are rude, while others are laid-back; some Buyers are conscious, while others are casual, which makes Selling difficult. As a result, businesses and salespeople must gain an understanding of each buyer category and prepare accordingly. The following are five broad categories of buyer types:

1. The Unplanned Buyers: These buyers have no set plan or schedule. We see them hovering around shops and supermarkets, and they are less likely to make a purchase. They'll likely make a purchase if they come across anything that piques their curiosity or if an appealing deal or special discount entices them. They are divided into two:

a. Mystery Shoppers: As the name implies, these are casual buyers who are often seen hovering and collecting information about the goods and services, quality, price, special deals, and other pertinent information. They don't buy in most cases, but their appearance and conversation make it seem like they will. They can purchase goods and services if they come across anything of interest or a good deal. They rarely purchase for various reasons, including an inability to afford now, seeking a better offer or deal, collecting information before purchasing, or simply browsing. Female shoppers, for example, visit several shops before making a purchase.

b. Bargain Hunters: These buyers are constantly on the lookout for a great price, a better deal, exclusive pricing, festival discounts, and so on. They want to save money by taking advantage of good sales and offers. In most cases, determining whether or not they can afford to purchase goods and services is challenging. They are more likely to purchase when reasonable prices, discounts, and offers are available. Off-season travelers, for example, search for great prices and offers.

2. Budget Buyers: These customers save their money before they have to spend it. They either have a set budget for purchasing goods and services or purchase only when they have a genuine need or need for certain goods and services. Instead of spending their money, these buyers prefer to keep it with them for as long as possible and invest it or save it. Before making a purchase, they measure and compare the value of the goods and services. They are classified into:

a. Need Buyers: These buyers only buy products and services when they have a genuine need or requirement. They are highly frugal with their money and only spend when necessary; otherwise, they save or invest it. People, for example, only purchase medication when they have a specific need or need.

b. Seasonal Buyers: These customers buy products and services on a seasonal or annual basis. They share the same characteristics as a Need Buyer in that they only spend when necessary. Purchasing seasonal clothing, for example, during the winter season.

3. Aggressive Buyers: When making a purchasing decision, these buyers are aggressive. They can be impulsive and make snap decisions at times, and they can also make the process complicated. It can be hard to manage and control these Buyers because they are often impulsive and lack crucial details. On the other hand, they become irritated and inquire excessively or become enraged about any important or unrelated problems. They are divided into two categories:

a. Impulsive Buyers: Impulsive buyers make decisions on the spur of the moment. These impulse purchases are typically unplanned, and they are made mainly based on enthusiasm, emotions, and feelings rather than logic. Limited-time sales, last-minute discounts, exceptional pricing, or product scarcity are only a few examples of impulse purchases. Purchasing an art piece at an auction, for example, necessitates a hasty decision.

b. Difficult Buyers: These buyers may become irritated with something and make the purchasing process difficult. They become violent in their words or deeds, erecting obstacles and wasting time and resources in the process. These buyers don't take it lightly and look for flaws or problems, causing problems. They irritate others by complaining about anything. For example, an irritated buyer can make the buying process more complicated by yelling and complaining.

4. Mindful Buyers: These buyers are well-informed and make informed decisions when purchasing products and services. These Buyers are similar to regular spenders, but they have more talents, experience, and expertise. They are well trained and can become active in the purchasing process and do extensive research before making a decision. They are divided into:

a. The Aware Customer is a serious buyer who is not in a rush. They take their time, looking for additional options or possibilities and thoroughly analyzing each one before making a buying decision. They may seek professional assistance if they are having trouble understanding or evaluating an opportunity, and they will always try to protect their interests by selecting the best product. Consider the case of an automobile engineer who is purchasing a vehicle.

b. The Bargaining Team: They are highly calculative and only spend when they think the product's price is reasonable and offers good value for money. They are average spenders trying to bargain in almost any case to get the best deal. They always research and compare all available information, choices, features, quality, and pricing of products and services before purchasing decisions. For example, a buyer negotiating the best price for a new or used vehicle.

5. The Spendthrift Buyers: These buyers are big spenders who have a hard time deciding what to buy. They are the polar opposite of Budget Spenders in that they believe in spending more and investing less. Rather than logic or reasoning, these consumers make purchases based on their emotions, thoughts, and interests. Emotions and feelings may influence their purchasing decisions based on advertising and marketing. They are classified into:

a. Sophisticated Buyers: When making a purchase, these buyers look for convenience, features, and benefits. They have outstanding product and service expertise and understanding. These buyers take their time and, if necessary, obtain additional details, ask more questions, and express concerns. They do extensive research, request a copy of the agreement and other related documents, and are fully aware of what they are purchasing. They value all relevant details exchanged, as well as the gathering of arrangement contracts and other documents. These buyers dislike being forced and need enough space during the buying decision-making process. Booking a cozy and luxurious resort for your next vacation, for example.

b. Affluent Buyers: These buyers make purchases based on their thoughts and emotions. They choose to purchase high-end goods that are exclusive. These buyers have limited time and take a short time to make a buying decision. An example is Purchasing an exclusive or limited edition luxury car.

These are a few of the Buyers' groups and types. When salespeople are aware of their buyer's category and style, it is much easier for them to establish stronger connections, rapport, and long-term business relationships.

CHAPTER 6: CHANGING BUYERS' ATTITUDES AND GETTING THEM TO BUY

By modifying a buyer's mindset, we mean influencing their thought process, rational thinking, and the emotional impulse to make a purchase decision. The buyer's mindset is the driving force behind their purchase decision.

A buyer's mindset is the guiding force behind any buying decision. Understanding why people buy certain goods or have desires for specific products or brands is the most critical business challenge. A salesperson wants to develop their products and services, tools and techniques, advertising and marketing, offer and profit, Sales Process, sales techniques, and relationship building. This further aids them in developing a more effective and profitable business model, which leads to the acquisition and retention of more clients.

Buyers Mindset and the degree of commitment they display when making a purchase determine their choices when purchasing products and services. For example, if the product's price is high, it will have a higher risk and a higher level of interaction. Some of the factors that influence a buyer's decision to buy are:

• **Engaged Buying Decision**: At this point, the buyer is very involved and conducts extensive research before purchasing. These goods typically carry a high level of financial, monetary, emotional, or psychological risk. Purchasing a home, luxury goods, luxurious watches, a luxury car, and choosing an educational course are just a few examples.

• **Logic-Based Purchasing Decision:** The Buyer conducts extensive analysis and remains active during the purchasing process, attempting to recognize all applicable product features and requirements as part of the offerings, down to the smallest detail, before making a buying decision. Consider purchasing a car, laptop, or phone after thoroughly researching all of its features and specifications.

• **Budget-Based Purchasing Decision:** The Buyer's main goal in this phase is to investigate the best choices available within the budget constraints. The ability to extend a budget is severely restricted. For example, buying a house for "X" sum of money, or monthly clothing or grocery expenses.

• **Habit-Based Purchasing:** In habit-based purchasing, the buyer makes no effort in making a decision and instead orders for their routine or daily choice. Purchasing a daily frappe at a coffee shop, a regular burger or pizza, or grocery shopping, for example.

• **Buying Decisions Based on Best Alternatives:** When identifying goods for purchase, buyers often choose the best available alternative if the product they want is not available, or even for the sake of trying out a new flavor. Buying Coke instead of Pepsi, for example, and vice versa.

• **Purchasing Decisions Based on Status:** When making a purchase, buyers often base their decision on their own or family's status. Unique or high-end luxury goods are purchased based on social standing. Purchasing a high-end luxury car or purchasing a business class airline ticket for flying.

• **Buying Decisions Based on the Feel Good or Look Good Factor:** Buyers often make purchasing decisions based on the feel-good or look good factor. This refers to when a customer purchases a product that makes them feel good about themselves or makes them look good after using it. Purchasing trendy clothing or attempting a beauty product or procedure to improve your appearance, for example.

• **Buying Decision Based on Variety**: When a buyer is searching for a variety of goods, flavors, and tastes, color, brand, etc., they look for variety in terms of different goods, flavors and tastes, color, brand, and so on. For instance, ordering various foods during a family picnic or purchasing a new pair of shoes, clothes, and accessories for various occasions.

• **Influence Dependent Purchasing Decisions**: When making a purchase, we decide based on external factors such as advertisement, promotion, marketing, offer guidance, and recommendation. For example, when ordering a burger and a soft drink, the Salesperson may recommend that the Buyer order a meal combo that includes the burger, soft drink, and fries, and the Buyer does so.

• **Buying Decisions Based on Enjoyment**: When purchasing a product, buyers often make decisions based on the fun factor. These types of purchases are typically made based on the buyer's hobby, curiosity, or entertainment. Purchasing a smartphone, guitar, sporting equipment, or participating in adventure sports, for example.

• **Buying Decisions Driven by Emotions**: Buying decisions are often influenced by our emotions, as they drive us. As a result, we base all of our decisions on our feelings. All purchase decisions are based on a combination of two or more factors, like emotions. Emotions, we may conclude, are essential factors in purchasing decisions.

These were only a few of the important considerations when making a purchase based on the Buyer's Mindset and Actions. Now we'll learn more about how to persuade the Buyer to make a purchase.

Buyer has a unique mindset, attitudes, and behaviors, and they adopt distinct trends in the selection and decision-making process when making a purchase. The decision to buy is made randomly, prepared, or determined based on these factors. Looking at the behavioral trends practiced during the transaction is a predictable mental design that is noticed, evaluated, and used to influence the Buyer in making a purchase. The following methods can be used to persuade buyers to make a purchase:

1. Promote the Brand, Products, and Services: Before making a purchase, the buyer researches different outlets such as supermarkets, websites, Google, Amazon, and others, so it is critical to promote the brand, products, and services. According to the adage "What is seen is sold," anything that has a stronger presence in the eyes of the buyers has a greater chance of persuading them to buy. For example, in any shop, items for children such as chocolate, cookies, candy, and toys are prominently displayed on lower shelves to attract children.

2. Advertisement, Marketing, and Promotion: Advertising, marketing, and promotion practices should be planned in such a way that they heavily affect the buyer's feelings, decisions, and mindset.

3. Buyers' Expectations: The primary goal is to comprehend the Buyer's needs and expectations. It is beneficial to consider the Buyer's viewpoint and how their Mindset influences their decision to buy when interacting with them. Pre-sales discussions with buyers to consider their requirements, desires, and expectations when purchasing a vehicle and using the information collected to provide solutions to fulfill these expectations can result in a quicker sale closing.

4. Objection Handling: During the pre-purchase meeting, the buyer should have questions, complaints, or grievances that must be adequately understood and answered. This is an opportunity for the Salesperson to establish a stronger connection with the Buyer, gain their trust and confidence, and influence their purchase decision. For example, handling and overcoming a home buyer's objections, demonstrating value, and providing solutions can contribute to a purchase.

5. Economic or Financial options: The economic or financial situation influences the purchasing decision. If the Buyer lacks the necessary funds to purchase the product or service, he or she will be hesitant to buy; however, providing financial options will influence and lead the Buyer to purchase. For example, in an electronic consumer product shop, if a buyer is looking for low-cost items, high-end items with EMI or no-cost financing options are offered, influencing and transforming the buyer's mindset and encouraging them to buy.

6. Relationship Selling: This has been viewed as a continuous process that begins with ease, confidence, rapport, and a relationship. The Salesperson acts as a Relationship Executive or Manager, interacting with the Buyer to learn about them, their needs and preferences, purchasing habits and mindset, and providing value-based solutions. Organizations assign Relation Managers to oversee their high-end or top clients in any industry, for example.

7. Testimonials and Reviews: Showing potential buyers positive testimonials and feedback from satisfied clients can greatly impact their mindset and purchasing decision. For example, almost every company employs this technique when making a presentation to a potential buyer, which results in a higher conversion rate.

8. Group Influence: Since humans are social creatures, they are affected by one another. As a result, this may be a great way to market goods and services to a small group of customers because if they buy, more will follow. Team sports, political advocacy, social movements, and public events, for example, all benefit from group impact.

9. Create scarcity: When there is a lack of a particular commodity on the market, people create more chaos and hype, resulting in intensive buying. This element greatly impacts the buyers' mindset and decision-making, making them want to purchase right away. When Covid-19 outbursts worldwide and a lockout are declared, people perceive this as a danger and a shortage issue for grocery goods, leading to widespread buying and hoarding.

10. Limited Time Deal: Companies use this tactic mostly during the holiday season to manipulate buyers' mindsets and decision-making, resulting in immediate purchases since the offer is only available for a limited time. For example, during festival season, a company may offer a steep discount for three or five days, and sometimes, a company may launch a limited edition offer of goods for select clients in limited quantities and a limited period.

11. Use Emotions to Engage Buyers: The best approach is to interact emotionally with the buyers and engage in buying decisions based on emotions. This aids in shaping their mindset and buying decisions. iPhone owners, for example, are ardent fans who are deeply invested in the brand and its products.

12. Satisfy their Egos: Buyers who make purchasing decisions will consider what they will benefit from purchasing. As a result of getting the upper hand in the buying process, the Buyer can develop egocentric tendencies. As a result, the Salesperson's job is to make the Buyer feel at ease, appease their ego, and contribute to a buying decision. Being constructive and polite with clients who have a strong ego and soothing and satisfying them by finding the right solutions, for example, can go a long way.

13. Clear their Fear of Loss: Buyers may be concerned that purchasing your product may result in them losing money or that it will not have the benefits claimed. This apprehension may result from a bad experience in the past, or it may be normal if the cost is high. By communicating well and discussing all of the Buyer's pain points, you will help them relax and become more relaxed, influencing their mindset and buying decision. For example, there are many fears associated with selecting the right education course; by approaching them one by one with all relevant details, previous track record, and alumni testimonials, all fears are removed, and the decision to choose is made.

14. Share Visual Elements and Success Stories: Sharing visual elements and success stories when choosing your goods and services is a powerful tool for convincing potential buyers. This aids in gaining a larger share of mind and influencing the buyer's mindset and decision-making. Sharing product features, updates, and success stories via newsletters, for example, is a great way to get buyers' attention and contribute to a purchase decision.

15. Create a Memorable Experience: For most buyers, buying can be a traumatic experience due to fear, anxiety, anger, emotional baggage, frustration, stress, mistrust, lack of response, and lack of support. As a result, Salespeople must engage with their Buyers from the beginning to the end of the buying process, making them feel at ease and enjoying the process and treating them well. When a buyer wants to buy a car, the salesperson can handle them well and show them all of the features, requirements, and value the car will provide. Make this a memorable journey for them, and it will affect their mindset and decision-making by causing them to buy and be happy with their choice.

These are a few of the highly successful and valuable techniques for manipulating buyers' mindsets and decision-making, contributing to purchases. The company and salesperson must consider the Buyer's expectations and requirements, evaluate them thoroughly, execute appropriate strategies, and act quickly. This will aid in shaping the buyers' mindset and decision-making and make them more likely to buy.

CHAPTER 7: HANDLING OBJECTIONS

During the presentation, the client may have questions, reservations, or even objections, all of which must be answered and dealt with accordingly. Suppose a client asks questions, inquiries, worries, or raises objections. In that case, it means the client is concerned about the problem and is interested in the product and services provided as a solution. This is a strong indication that the client is thinking about or is likely to think about the approach you've proposed.

As a Highly Skilled Salesperson, you must accept the client's objections, pay close attention to them, perceive them simply, and treat them with tact. You must explain and satisfactorily overcome every objection, which will lead to Sales Closure.

Objection 1: Price

When dealing with client objections, you must persuade the client of the product's and services' advantages, improved efficiency, and significant results. When dealing with objections, you must demonstrate the intrinsic and essential qualities of intelligence, skills, competence, and patience to overcome all objections and turn them into sales.

- Ask Question: Okay, I understand why you would say that, but is there something else on your mind besides Price?
- Pose a question: If price or budget isn't an issue, can our products and services assist you in solving your problem?
- Give Value: The following are the qualities that our products and services have to offer. Values should be shared.
- If an instant offer is available, make it: Will you be willing to buy right now if we offered you 10% off? Alternatively, you might give them the option of paying in installments.

Objection 2: Lack of Interest or Urgency

These are typical objections clients may have due to a lack of interest, a lack of decision-making, a lack of urgency, or the possibility of a deal being delayed. To answer the following statements or queries, clients may use statements such as "I am not interested," "Send me details to review," "Call me next month or quarter," "This is not the right time to start," and so on. The following statements or questions may be used to answer them:

• Pose a question: "Sure, before that, can I ask you a few questions so that I can better understand how we can assist?"

• Ask and Provide Value: "I understand you are busy right now. I'd like to show you how we can help you 'reduce your cost by 20%,' 'improve your processes or product output by 20%,' or 'create value through our product or services,' so that we can talk again at a convenient time and discuss further."

• Ask and Provide Value: "I'd be happy to share details with you, but first, could we have a short demo of our goods and services to see if we can add value to your organization? If you're interested, we'll gladly tailor our offer to better meet your needs; sound fair?"

• Demonstrate concern and provide value: That's fine; I didn't expect you to be interested right away, but I'm confident that learning how our goods and services will help you increase sales force efficiency by 20-30% would pique your interest."

Objection 3: Competition-Related objection

There are typical objections clients may have about your competition, such as having used their product before, comparing your product to theirs, and so on. The following questions or statements can be used to answer common objections: "We are already negotiating with another business," "We have a binding contract, we can't alter," "I am getting a better or cheaper deal from the competition," "I am satisfied with my vendor," and so on. To address these objections, you can use the following questions or statements:

• Pose a question: "I understand your point, but may I ask you how your experience with your supplier or vendor has been so far?"

• Inquire and provide value: "Great to hear; could I share a case study of one of our clients who were able to "reduce 20% expense" or "increase 20% revenue" by moving from XYZ company (Competitor's name) to our solutions?"

• Offer Value: "Thank you for sharing/telling; I'd like to take this opportunity to show you how we can help our customers 'reduce their costs by 20%' or 'increase revenue by 20%' despite the fact that our price is higher than XYZ Company (competitor)".

Objection 4: objections Related to Product and Service Quality

These are common objections clients may have about product and service quality, or they may have doubts about it or have heard it from others. Popular comments include "I need to think about it," "I'm not sure if this will meet our needs," "I've had a bad experience with similar products or services," "I don't understand your product," "I don't see any appeal to me or my business," "I'm not sure if your product will last," and so on. To answer these objections, you can ask the following questions and make the following statements:

• Inquire: "Would you mind if I inquire as to what specific needs you are seeking or believe you might need in terms of product or services?"

• Inquire and Provide Value: "Clients who use our goods or services find it more useful to see the solution in action. Would you like to see a short demo? Often, share the high-quality aspects of your goods and services."

• Offer Value: "I'd like to share with you that by using our supply chain application and software, XYZ Company was able to minimize their operation, expense, and time consumption, resulting in a 20% cost reduction."

Objection 5: Authority or Decision Objecting

These are typical objections clients can have, such as procrastination, fear of making decisions, or uncertainty about either of the above objections. "I need to discuss with my staff, wife, partners, other stakeholders, or board of directors" is a typical argument. This objection may be legitimate, or customers may use it to procrastinate, stall decisions, or cheat you out. You may use the following questions and statements to respond to these objections:

• Pose a question: "That makes a lot of sense; do you think he/she/they may have any additional questions about our discussion?" "What kinds of questions would he/she/they have to ask?" if yes. If you dig a little deeper here, you could find out what the client is hiding, which might be due to price or quality objections, among other things.

• Pose a question: "I see. Let me ask you two questions: First, what do you think the most compelling reason for them to choose our solution is?" and two, what do you think the most important reason they won't accept our answer is?"

• Pose a question: "Thank you for your support; given our conversation thus far and the fact that you'd like us to collaborate, based on your experience, how soon do you think you'll get the sign-off?"

• Request that the client includes the decision-maker: "I completely understand that you need to talk with them, so if it's okay with you, I'll be happy to reach out to him/her/them (decision-makers) directly and answer any questions he/she/they might have, will that be okay with you and him/her/them?"

Objection 6: Other Factors Involved

Clients may have other objections, such as "They don't know you," "They don't trust you," "They had a poor experience with your company," "They are closing their operations or downsizing," or "They are changing their line of business." You will demonstrate value by sharing testimonials and experiences from other businesses you've represented and benefited by asking more open-ended and follow-up questions to understand their issue and answer it appropriately.

How to Handle All Objections

These were the most common objections that a client may have. As a Highly Skilled Salesperson, you must pursue a step-by-step method in Handling Objections, and you must use specific tactics or skills during this process. These measures and techniques are incredibly effective throughout the process:

• Be Still, Take a Pause, and Speak: When dealing with objections, you should remain calm, take a brief pause to demonstrate that you are paying attention, and then speak with complete clarity, speech, and thinking. It allows you to have more time to reflect, understand, and react.

• Demonstrate Empathy: Demonstrate empathy and use terms that demonstrate empathy when speaking or reacting.

It aids in establishing a stronger connection with the customer.

• With each objection, ask a question: Asking questions is the only way to address the objection. It will assist in determining the true objection or concern that the client may have.

• Validate Objections: When you're posing a question, you need to communicate with the client to move the discussion forward and make it more relevant. To keep the conversation going, you can ask follow-up questions about their previous statement or response. Until responding, you must first explain, enquire, and verify the objection.

• Distinguish between Objections: Often, the client's initial opposition isn't the actual objection, or the client will have to pose further objections when probing or validating them; you'll need to differentiate them and reconfirm for the nearest or most correct one. It assists in identifying and addressing the appropriate objection.

• Request Permission Before Proposing a Solution: When requesting permission, ask how the client feels in control and has authority. The aim is to present the idea to your client to elicit interest and interaction to obtain their feedback. You can say things like, "Can I bounce some ideas off you before we continue?" or "Can I share a few thoughts with you?"

• Use Synonyms and Antonyms: To alter the tone, context, or effect of a sentence, you can need to use unfamiliar words or synonyms. The sentence can become more effective and optimistic by changing a term. Similarly, you might need to use Antonyms or opposite terms to lessen the impact of the objections to negate the impact of the sentence. • Using Synonyms: If a client says, "Your product is very expensive," the impact of the word expensive is reduced by using synonyms and reconfirming the objection, such as, "Ok, I understand why you might say that; is there anything else that worries you?"

• By using antonyms: If a client says, "We are experiencing a pandemic across the country; right now is the worst time to start something," the effect of the word "worst" is negated by using different words and sentences such as "Because business is slowing across the country, right now is not a good time for this project."

• Demonstrate Value: Emphasize the value proposition and demonstrate how your goods and services are superior and can solve your client's dilemma. Once you've identified your client's pain points, ask the right question to match your beliefs with their suffering. Demonstrate how pain can cost an organization money in various ways, including increased costs, sales loss, time spent, customer frustration, employee turnover, missed opportunities, and so on. You will empower the client to measure and turn these values into business and development by aligning these pain points with value.

• Share Social Proof to Back It Up: You must share market analysis, customer testimonials or references, and their success stories using your goods and services to back up your arguments and statements. You may use industry experts' reports and opinions, as well as their written reports on the industry, your product, and services. This will aid in the creation of authenticity and serve as social evidence. Client testimonials of similar objections and the advantages they received after implementing the solutions.

• Impartial Resolution and Follow-Up: The final move is to settle the objection using an unbiased approach and follow-up. This means ensuring that the client's objection or concern has been answered and resolved to their satisfaction before moving on to the next step of the sales process.

If you've successfully handled an objection, you'll move on to the next phase in the sales process, which is Agreement and Acknowledgement.

CHAPTER 8: SKILLS NEEDED TO MASTER THE ART OF SELLING 1: NEGOTIATION

Have you ever noticed that you negotiate with your spouse, family, friends, neighbors, colleagues, bosses, people on the road, people in the workplace, your clients, and even yourself daily? Yes, you do negotiate every day, with everybody, everywhere. Simply put, life is a series of negotiations.

You engage in several negotiations from the moment you wake up to the time you retire to bed, and you are completely unaware of it. And much of the time, it is done subconsciously, but sometimes it is done consciously, and when it is done consciously, you notice it.

Five more minutes of sleep, not eating properly, rushing late to work, bargaining with a taxi, contract terms and conditions, performance discussion, fee payment, defining deadlines, hiring for a job, firing from a job, partnership, and joint ventures, business consolidation, making offers, agreement, settlement, purchasing an asset, etc.

You are a Negotiator in all of the above cases, whether you like it or not. You are a part of Negotiation, and you deal with it at home, outside, or at work, wherever you go or do.

Negotiation is usually described as "a process of strategic dialogue between two or more people or parties over a conflict, matter, or situation to resolve it agreeably and satisfactorily to all of the people or parties." Each participant in the negotiation attempts to convince others to agree with their point of view or obtain a leading position. However, at the close of the negotiation, to avoid a stalemate, an amicable conclusion si reached by deciding on some sort of agreement.

"Negotiation is a mechanism in which two or more parties meet to resolve a dispute by reaching mutual agreements and compromise," according to another definition.

The following are the basic principles of negotiation:

• Be calm and comfortable in uncertain and contradictory circumstances.

• In Negotiation, parties have at least some mutual interest in the exchange of Offers. • Being mindful of the transaction's underline, product, facilities, laws, choices, alternatives, opportunities, and risks.

• In general, the result is hampered by the parties' differing viewpoints and objectives.

• The parties agree and consider negotiation to be a more effective means of resolving their differences.

• Each group is confident in their ability to convince the other to obtain an advantage.

• Each negotiation necessitates compromise or a shift of perspective to achieve an appropriate agreement.

• Finally, the parties recognize their respective positions and cooperate for the mutual benefit of both parties, aiming for a win-win situation.

• Possess market insight and the ability to detect secret agendas and opportunities.

• Have the confidence to inquire and probe for the details you need, then double-check your answers.

Negotiation Strategy Types

Distributive and Integrative Negotiation are two types of negotiation strategies that are used in the negotiation process. Depending on the Negotiator's attitude or the circumstances, these strategies may be used. The majority of negotiations incorporate aspects of both forms of negotiations. It's critical to comprehend and analyze how both forms are used:

1. Distributive Negotiation

Parties in Distributive Negotiation negotiate over a single topic, usually price or profit. Positional or Competitive or Fixed Pie or Win Loose Negotiation, in which parties fight for a large share of the pie, is another name for this type of negotiation. Distributive Negotiation entails having a conversation and advocating for a fixed concept, or position, of what you want, regardless of any underlying interests.

Distributive negotiation, also known as positional or hard-bargaining negotiating, results in one party receiving a larger share of the pie. Divorce is a typical example of Distributive Negotiation, in which one party takes control of the other's properties and money.

This approach is primarily concerned with achieving immediate objectives without regard for potential relationships. The parties usually expend the least amount of time and resources available to settle the dispute because there are no new innovative solutions. The aim is to achieve a fast outcome by presenting fixed options and making decisions and choices as quickly as possible.

2. Integrative Negotiation

In Integrative Negotiation, parties are simultaneously negotiating on several issues. They can make tradeoffs around issues and build value when several issues are addressed. This negotiation aims to balance various issues with the shared goal of achieving a win-win situation. Cooperative, Interest-based, Merit-based, Non-zero Sum, Win-Win, or Principled Negotiation are all terms used to describe Integrative Negotiation.

In this negotiation, the parties work together to reach a mutually beneficial agreement. Both parties have a win-win mentality regarding drawing a decision or result that benefits both of them, and they walk away pleased and fulfilled. Salary Negotiation, for example, covers a wide range of topics, including salary, venue, travel expenses, housing, insurance, paid and unpaid leaves, increments, bonuses, and much more.

Negotiation's Potential Outcomes

People always think of negotiation as a process with a single goal: to win, but this dynamic process can have several different outcomes. Negotiation can result in a variety of outcomes depending on many factors. For example, the parties' position, strengths, weaknesses, main transaction or agreement, the situation, the price or cost, the offerings, the product or service need and demand, the willingness and interest to participate, and so on. These outcomes can be described as follows:

1. **Surrender: I Lose - You Win:** When you are in a weaker position than your opponent, this outcome occurs. If you're

a small supplier supplying a large store, for example, you'll need to negotiate their price and conditions.

2. Command: I Win – You Lose: When you are in a stronger position than your opponent, this outcome occurs. For example, suppose you own a monopoly and sell goods at your own price and terms.

3. Trade-Off: I Lose – You Lose: When either party concedes a negotiating role outside of their goal range, this outcome occurs. Both sides end up in a worse situation, resulting in a Lose-Lose situation. This situation can emerge due to either a refusal to make concessions or haste to make concessions; either situation can result in this outcome. Both sides are often involved in such cases because they can make a bargain despite the consequences. For example, labor unions refuse to return to work if their demands are not heard and resolved, while management refuses to listen until labor unions return to work. For both sides, this results in a Lose-Lose situation.

4. Tie or Stalemate: No Win – No Lose: When no side wins or loses, this outcome occurs. Even after a long negotiation, both sides are back where they began, which often happens because neither party is interested in or can compromise. Both parties act aggressively in this situation to protect their position and to break the other side. For example, in a conflict situation, where both sides cannot listen or make concessions, the result is a No Win – No Lose situation.

5. Agreement: I Win – You Win: This is the most desired outcome in every negotiation. In this case, both sides will carry out their least viable option and are prepared to find a fair middle ground to help both parties. Both sides work well together to identify innovative new ways that strengthen their respective positions and interests. As a result, a win-win scenario emerges. For instance, consider a job offer negotiation that results in a win-win situation for both parties.

These are all Potential Negotiation Outcomes between two or more parties. Each group comes to the negotiation with its own agenda and expectations. They arrive at an outcome or result based on the expectations of both or all parties.

Negotiation Stages and Techniques to Use at each stage

Negotiation aims to reach an agreement/situation where both sides are happy with the outcome or outcomes. We can divide the negotiation process into four stages, and by using specific techniques in each stage, you can succeed in any negotiation. These Stages and Techniques can be defined as follows:

1. **Preparation Stage**

This is the first and most important stage in the negotiation process. Determine all planning you need to do before getting on the table, depending on the type and condition of the negotiation. Techniques for successful training include the following:

Gather Information: This technique involves gathering all relevant information before the meeting. You must learn everything you can about the problem, situation, opportunities, risks, and issues involved, and plan as much as possible.

Research on People Involved: It is important to understand the people involved in the negotiation and conduct a thorough investigation into each of them. As a negotiator, you should be aware of their negotiation style, temperament, weaknesses, and strengths.

Improve Your BATNA: This technique aims to get to know yourself better, assess your situation, and determine your best options. You must plan ahead of time, know what you want, and be prepared to deal with any objections that might arise. Knowing the Value Offered and Alternatives available will help you improve your BATNA.

Meeting Location: In this strategy, you can strive to make the meeting location your own. This gives you an edge since you are familiar with the atmosphere and can manage it if necessary. Otherwise, try and fix a common place that you are familiar with, such as a restaurant or a club, or you can go there and spend some time there and chat with their staff and become more relaxed and use them to your advantage.

2. **Engaging in Conversation**

The parties involved in the negotiation meet and present themselves at this point. The goal is to establish rapport and begin the negotiation process by engaging and sharing clear communication or details. The strategies used in this stage are as follows:

Meet and Greet: In this technique, begin a conversation by schmoozing (informal chat) because it aids in the development of instant Connect and Rapport.

Knowledge Sharing: In this method, all parties exchange information about the contract, their understanding, and any questions they may have. It's difficult to evaluate all of the options and alternatives you and the other party have on the table to explore and negotiate without all sides providing relevant details.

Learn to Play with Emotions: Use your Emotional Intelligence to take command of every situation. People act in such ways in specific situations and circumstances; try to spot them and exploit them. You should also be able to regulate your own emotions.

Active Listening: This approach requires you to use one of your listening, observing, and expressing skills in a nonverbal way of communication. You can use your stance, facial expression, eye contact, body movement, and sometimes repeat the last word said by the other person or use terms like "yes," "agree," "I see," "correct," and so on, as well as ask questions when necessary. These things contribute to expressing that you are committed and understanding, and allowing others to talk contributes to a stronger bond and connection, leading to a better relationship and rapport.

3. The Bargaining Phase

This is the point at which you're getting closer to your goals, which laid the groundwork for the negotiation. The goal is to convince the other party that your demand is reasonable compared to the value or offer you have. The strategies used in this stage are as follows:

Make the First Bid: This strategy aims to start the negotiation by making a first offer, which is normally the lease that the other party prefers. However, it brings a zing to the bargaining process.

Re-analyze Options and BATNA: This approach consists of simply observing and re-analyzing the Options and BATNA. The aim is to examine your current strengths, weaknesses, and status. It aids in defining new areas for bargaining and directing the flow in your favor.

Use the Push and Pull Technique: In this technique, you play with your emotions by expressing your interest in one topic while expressing your frustration or aggression in another. It causes other parties to be perplexed, and they feel pressured and uncertain about the situation. Positively influencing your choice.

Express Value, Strength, and Confidence: This technique aims to express your values, strength, and confidence in your current stance. It aids in putting pressure on the other party and gives you an advantage.

4. Agreement closure

All sides have reached the final stage of the negotiation process when they reach an agreement to close. They're about to talk about the final terms and conditions before signing a legally binding agreement. This leads to the agreement being closed, with both sides achieving a win-win situation. The strategies used in this stage are as follows:

Adhere to Fair Negotiation Standards: By using this strategy, you must adhere to Fair Negotiation Standards and be frank, cooperative, polite, and fair to your counterparty. All parties must work together to bring the situation to a mutually satisfactory end and resolution.

Complement their Negotiation Skills: You must complement the other party's negotiating skills in this technique. This gesture would assist in making them feel at ease, fulfilled, and confident in their performance. This makes it more likely that they will agree on most of the terms and sign the contract.

Finalize the Terms of Agreement: In this technique, all parties agree to the final terms and conditions of the contract. The goal is to draft a formal contract or agreement that details every aspect of the transaction. It aids in the faster and more effective solidification of the Agreement.

Lead to Close Win-Win: In this strategy, both sides take the lead in bringing the agreement to a successful conclusion in a Win-win situation that benefits both parties. It aids in the development of stronger relationships, confidence, and bonds for future business.

These are the Stages of the Negotiation Process. At each stage, a few tactics are used to bring the agreement to a close, find a compromise, or resolve a dispute. Negotiation is a powerful skill to learn, and it is helpful in a variety of relationships, including family, friends, colleagues, and company.

CHAPTER 9: SKILLS NEEDED TO MASTER THE ART OF SELLING 2: PERSUASION

"Persuasion is a method of communication used to persuade the individual to say 'Yes to your offer," according to the simplest meaning.

Persuasion is one of the most common and valuable techniques used in daily life, and it is one of the many skills required to be a Highly Effective Salesperson. Many circumstances arise where you must persuade someone to change their minds, approve or agree to your plan, or purchase what you are selling without difficulty. You will succeed if you can persuade them.

In daily life, you either convince others or are convinced by others, whether consciously or unconsciously. Persuasion is a skill that can be mastered by preparation, planning, practice, and persistence. It is a skill that can be acquired through interactions, training, or practice.

Persuasion aims to influence, inspire, or alter your counterparty or audience through verbal and nonverbal communication. Persuasion is a very important skill that can be used implicitly or explicitly, and it can have both positive and negative consequences. As a result, persuasion should be used ethically and constructively to persuade or influence people to accept your point of view, follow your viewpoints, agree with you, and change their attitude or behavior.

Persuasion Principles for Influencing People

Reciprocation

The Giving and Taking... Reciprocity is the fundamental concept that expresses our basic human existence of repaying favors and treating others as we wish to be treated. We mean reciprocity when we say we'll take a chance and give something to people, and they'll feel obligated to return the favor by offering something in return. It's a type of mutual expectation that involves a give-and-take relationship. When a person gives something to another, it is a form of power that allows the recipient to be influenced. Similarly, in business, when you go above and beyond for a customer, they appreciate it and return the favor by giving you more business. Reciprocity aids in developing others' trust and faith in you, contributing to a stronger business partnership.

Hobgoblins of the Mind

Commitment and Consistency This principle is extremely effective because if the other person or client has agreed to do something, it becomes an issue of pride, authority, and strength, and they follow through. However, whether the pledge is made verbally or casually, people are more likely to back out. Consequently, the pledge must be written down or performed in front of others for people to follow through with their words of commitment. When anyone makes a written or verbal commitment, they are more likely to follow through. They do so, though, because other people see it, which brings responsibility to their dedication and implementation. The first step in persuading others to do something is to get them to make certain types of commitments, which leads to continuity in their behavior when dealing with you.

Social Proof: We Are Truths

This principle states that people consider and depend on social signals from others to determine how they think, feel, and act in certain cases. People are naturally drawn to observe what others are doing, both consciously and subconsciously, and this is a form of embracing and reciprocating behavior known as Social Proof. People, for example, always choose the more crowded restaurant over the one that is more silent, even though they must wait a long time for their turn because they believe the crowded restaurant is better and serves better food. To demonstrate Social Proof, a company or organization shows or talks about how many happy customers they have, how many items they have sold, how many projects they have completed, and their clients' celebrities. We can also do this through customer testimonials, third-party ratings, and references.

Liking

The Friendly Thief: According to Cialdini's principle, people are easily persuaded by people they like. People are easily persuaded and more likely to buy from people or organizations they like. This feeling of likeness may be conscious or subconscious, and you might be completely unaware of it. Getting something in common or similarities with each other is one of the most important aspects of like. For example, to create a stronger relationship with your client, you must learn more about that individual, such as sports, movies, academics, likes, hobbies, and preferences.

Authority: Directed Deference

This is one of Cialdini's most powerful principles, which states that people obey the orders of authority figures such as government officials, teachers, saints, professionals, doctors, specialists, and consultants, who are experts in their field, whether consciously or subconsciously. People value authority, and they believe that if an Authority Figure is affiliated with a company or organization as a spokesperson or brand ambassador, people will support the brand or organization and become customers. For example, both brands use movie or television stars, models, and athletes as brand ambassadors, which results in an immediate increase in the number of clients who look up to or admire these celebrities.

Scarcity

This is a powerful principle that states that scarce and difficult-to-get items can draw more customers to want them. People believe or presume that products that aren't readily available have higher value and are better than those that are. For instance, a hotel booking site can display a limited number of rooms available in a hotel; this shortage is used to persuade customers to act quickly. "Only a few days," "Offer expiring on," "Limited time offer," "Limited edition," "Only a few seats available," and so on are some other examples. These examples generate a sense of scarcity for the product or service, prompting customers to move quickly or risk losing such a lucrative deal.

Unity

This Principle is all about a sense of belonging. This theory expresses our desire to belong to a faith, culture, party, or family, among other things. When people become members of a group, they develop a sense of belonging, and they feel bigger, stronger, and more united in these groups. People inquire about their likes and dislikes, hobbies, where they came from, where they are going, which sports they play, who their favorite athlete or actor is, and so on when they meet for the first time to know themselves better and identify what they have in common. This theory aids in forming a bond, a link, or a sense of belonging to a community with similar interests, needs, and preferences. To make the most of this powerful principle, look for similarities between you and your client and have a discussion about them to establish a connection and rapport. You may apply this principle by incorporating or providing premium services such as an exclusive lounge, club, or membership, which will allow customers to categorize themselves and select such plans or deals more easily.

Other Effective People-Influencing Principles:

Request a Small Favor

This is one of the most powerful principles because when you ask for small favors, people seldom say no and are willing to help. Once they provide small assistance, they become more accessible or crack the ice.

Express Interest

This Principle is all about showing genuine interest in someone's qualities, hobbies, background, stories, life, career, family, or anything else. This can be accomplished by posing pertinent questions and truly listening to the answers. It leads to a stronger connection, bonding, and rapport, which attracts others to your powerful magnetic force, allowing you to persuade them further. For example, when showing your client watches, asking questions, and taking an interest in learning about their likes and dislikes, hobbies, sports, or anything else you can associate with and show anything that matches the theme would result in a faster sale of a premium product.

Compliment Sincerely

Positive and happy feelings are evoked by complementing, contributing to confidence and attachment. Complementing takes little more than a moment of thought, and when done correctly, it will work well for you. For example, when showing your client a bracelet, compliment them on their wrist and tell them you have something special for their lovely hands, and this will lead to a sale.

Infuse Energy

When you encounter someone, your energy level either increases or decreases. This is dependent on the person. If the other person is inspired, energized, and laughing, he or she will raise your energy level, making you feel motivated and excited as well. Eye contact, a smile or humor, physical touch, a verbal response, or even active listening may all contribute to this. You have a strong bond with that individual. For example, when you board an airplane, you are greeted with a warm smile by Air Hostesses, which increases your energy level and excitement.

Share a Secret or Deep Truth

To create a stronger bond with your audience or customer, you can tell them about your past journey, how you struggled and tried again to get to where you are now, or you can tell them the deep truth about themselves that no one else can tell them. Giving your secret to others and telling them the truth about you is the most challenging job, but if done correctly and without being judgmental or having a hidden agenda, this Principle will help you create confidence and more communication, which leads to positive responses.

Trust and Credibility

Many people believe that trust and credibility are associated with names, brands, etc., but the truth is that trust and credibility are earned and built over time. Trust and credibility are essential components of any successful business relationship. It is simple to persuade a client once trust and credibility have been built. Doctors in Health Care Products, for example, bring more Confidence and Credibility to the products and services provided.

Remind Them of Their Fear

Fear is one of the most powerful psychological tools for persuasion. Most insurance and quit-smoking, alcohol, and drug-abuse advertisements attempt to terrify people, and they succeed most of the time. Fear is a powerful tool for persuasion, but it must be combined with a solution to be even more efficient. For example, highlighting the dangers of bad oral hygiene among children by stating the negative consequences and how to address the issue is a good way to persuade children to practice good oral hygiene.

15. Communicate Urgency: The Principle of Urgency communicates feelings of urgency to act rapidly. When you believe that whatever is going on is extremely critical and only available for a limited time, urgent action is needed. As a result, you must instill a sense of urgency in the minds of your clients or others for them to act quickly. People are more likely to act quickly if there is a sense of urgency created by a lack of time, limited stock, or a special price. For example, most trainers now give substantial discounts on their training programs if you act quickly.

16. Confidence is Contagious: This Principle emphasizes the value of self-assurance. People are drawn to and persuaded by others who are self-assured or seem to be so. It's difficult to tell if anyone is faking it because it's so difficult to tell. Confidence is the product of several important factors, including your level of preparedness, understanding, intelligence, experience, how you dress, your body language, and the use of powerful words with the appropriate tone and smile. During the communication or sales process, projecting trust by listening, verbal communication, or body language assists in putting the customer at ease. Confidence is a soft skill that can be learned, developed, refined, and improved with the proper education, training, and practice.

17. Eliminate All Doubts: This Principle of Certainty is extremely useful in removing any doubts that others may have about you, your product, or your services. Certainty is a form of conviction that leaves no room for doubt or skepticism. Certainty can be compelling and intoxicating when it comes to persuading others to be drawn to them, their products, services, or solutions. E.g., suppose you are selling a vacation package to a customer. In that case, you can persuade them by saying, "Dear Mr. XYZ, because you are aware that Summers is rapidly approaching and it is certain that the cost of Tour Packages and Flight Tickets will skyrocket if you book now, I will help you save at least 30-40% of the total cost."

18. Persistence Pays Off: Persistence is one of the most effective principles in persuasion because it is the willingness of an individual to continue pursuing an objective or desired outcome even in the face of adversity, even when you realize it will take a long time and energy. This holds everywhere, but it is particularly true in sales. According to research, a customer typically says "no" at least 4-5 times before saying "yes" for the final time, and most salespeople abandon follow-up after 2-3 times. Still, a Highly Effective Salesperson manage to follow up and close the deal. The best way forward is to keep track of your customer and demonstrate the value you have. This is the ultimate persuasion strategy that leads to further sales.

19. Ask to Introduce / Refer: When you ask a current customer to introduce their family and friends to sell your goods and services or solutions, you can have a greater effect because you are approaching them through someone they have confidence and trust. For example, suppose you're selling investment products and supporting your client for a while and have provided him with good returns and built a good rapport and relationship when you ask for a recommendation or introduction. In that case, they'll refer you to a friend, and you'll make more sales with less follow-up and effort.

20. Guarantee

This is the most effective persuasion technique since every customer wants a guarantee or warranty from the product, services, or offers. There are some words and phrases that everybody finds appealing and persuasive. Salespeople sometimes use them to sell more or close more deals. Money-back guarantee, 100 percent refund with no questions asked, Guaranteed Returns, Replacement Warranty, and so on.

These principles should be applied because they are highly effective and can be beneficial in any case. Since they circumvent our conscious or logical mind, these concepts are strong and valuable in most cases. Not only can these principles lead to sales, but they also lead to customer retention and loyalty.

The Method of Persuasion

Persuasion is a step-by-step negotiation mechanism aimed at persuading or influencing others. To make this a successful operation, the speaker or presenter should concentrate on the receivers or audience. The speaker must successfully engage his audience to convince them. The following are the steps in the persuasion process:

• **Step 1: Be Prepared and Know Your Audience**

Being prepared and knowing your audience is the first and most critical step in the persuasion process. For greater impact and reputation, you should thoroughly plan or rehearse your topic and have some statistics and data on hand. You must also understand who your target audience is and what expectations they might have.

• **Step 2: Get Attention and Establish Credibility**

The second step aims to get your audience's attention and establish credibility. You have 5-7 seconds to create a connection with your audience by being optimistic, making eye contact, smiling, using appropriate hand movements, and expressing emotions and empathy. You must state the intent of the discussion and tell your audience what to expect from the presentation or discussion to establish credibility.

You can increase confidence by using storytelling and humor, as well as facts, figures, and statistics.

• **Step 3: Creating a Common Ground Framework**

This phase aims to find areas of agreement between you and your audience. Persuasion is most successful when you emphasize the advantages to the people you're trying to persuade. To do this, you must first comprehend your audience's desires, expectations, interests, fears, issues, and challenges, and then change your stance until you and your audience share common ground. Once you understand the audience's information and facts, you can frame your stories and discussion topics accordingly. This will keep the audience on the same page and make them feel more connected, engaged, and trustworthy.

Step 4: Dominate your Audience with Distinctive Language and Social Proof

This move aims to compel the Audience to embrace your point of view by using or sharing data, figures, stories, metaphors, analogies, vivid phrases, or pictures to dominate or reinforce your role. The purpose is to prove value and explain the advantages of the products and services you're selling. People are more likely to be convinced if you have facts or social proof that your idea works. People place a higher value on emotional evidence like social proof, including testimonials, stories, and personal experiences. To convince their audience, good persuaders combine logic or reason with emotions.

Step 5: Empathically Communicate with Audience

This step aims to create a link with your audience, which can be accomplished by using emotions and empathy. To persuade the audience, you must strike a balance between professionalism and emotions and use empathy. People make decisions based on emotions and empathy, so good persuaders sense their audience's emotional state and change their tone and strength of their speech or argument accordingly. Persuaders learn to use their audience's role to adapt it to the same degree and speed to get their audience to receive the message and respond in the way they want.

Step 6: Make an Offer and a Call to Action

This step aims to close the deal. Now that you've addressed all objections, agreed with your audience's interests, and given suggestions and advantages, the next step is to make an offer/deal and then ask them to take action. Tell the audience the next line of action to get them to act as soon as possible. The goal is to close the deal quickly; otherwise, the audience can become distracted by something else, defeating the goal. You should end the presentation on a high note and continue to persuade the audience by reminding them what they will gain if they want to participate and what they will lose if they do not. Also, remind them that this is a limited-time deal or exclusive offer that might not be valid for a certain period. This will help to convince people by creating a sense of urgency and scarcity, which will lead to people closing quickly and closing further.

Persuasion is a crucial skill used in daily life, whether consciously or unintentionally, in personal and professional contexts. One can improve this ability and use it to their advantage in any situation by studying, practicing, and persevering.

CHAPTER 10: SKILLS NEEDED TO MASTER THE ART OF SELLING 3: COMMUNICATION

The word "communication" comes from the Latin word "communicare," which means "to share" or "to participate." This is the act of interacting with another person by using signs, signals, symbols, or phrases that both parties clearly understand.

Any animal or race's life and survival are contingent on communication. Members of any species, culture, or group communicate with one another by sharing their opinions, ideas, knowledge, feelings, facts, and messages. The goal or purpose of any conversation in communication is to create or improve connections and understanding among all community members.

Communication may seem simple, but it is a dynamic process that necessitates excellent and highly effective communication skills. These abilities are highly sought after in every field, including sales. You must learn to communicate in a precise, effective, and unambiguous manner understood by all parties involved.

Personal conversations, text calls, emails, letters, magazines, newspapers, television, radio, and social networking are all examples of modes or media used in communication. Individuals and groups may use it to talk, exchange information, send messages, and express emotions.

Communication is important in any organization because it allows for the flow of knowledge and clear understanding between people in similar or different departments and senior management to lower management. The flow of information is crucial for administrative effectiveness and the smooth operation of all departments and organizations. Since communication occurs across various channels or layers, it is critical to retain the message or information in its original form and ensure that it is clearly understood by all when being disseminated.

When used properly, communication may aid in a better understanding of people, eliminating all misunderstandings, and facilitating the unity of thinking and speech between individuals, groups, or departments within an organization. It assists in bridging the distance between people and bringing them closer together.

Communication may take place in both formal and informal settings:

1. Formal Communication

This type of communication is conducted via a formal channel within the company. This communication may take the form of either oral or written communication. This information is generally communicated in a logical order, such as vertically or horizontally. Horizontal communication flows between departments, while vertical communication flows from top to bottom or vice versa. For example, sending an email to a client introducing yourself and requesting an appointment, sharing meeting minutes, sharing product writeups and proposals, and so on.

2. Informal Communication

This type of communication is carried out via an unofficial channel within the company. This form of communication is referred to as "grapevine" communication. In informal conversation, information is often skewed and disseminated quickly, and it is often referred to as gossip. To engage a client effectively, you will need to address topics relevant to their interests to develop a stronger relationship and rapport. These subjects may be about their interests, life experiences, business news, or political news in general.

Communication may take the form of verbal, written, or behavioral means, for example:

i. Verbal Communication: This is communication performed either verbally or orally and may be formal or informal. For example, in a meeting with a client, the entire conversation is verbal, so you must master the art of verbal communication.

ii. Written Communication: Emails, memos, messages, and media / social media releases are examples of formal written communication. For instance, structured written correspondence with a client in which you introduce yourself, share other relevant details, and so on.

iii. Nonverbal communication: This type of communication takes the form of signs, movements, nods, acts, phrases, indicators, and facial expressions and is commonly used in informal settings. When interacting with a client, it is beneficial to use hand motions, body expression, mirroring, and coordinating with the client's movements.

The Importance of Sales Communication

In sales, communication is crucial because it allows you to communicate more effectively with your client and ensures that orders and details are clear. This aids in developing a stronger bond and understanding with customers, which increases the likelihood of a sale being closed.

• **Flow of Information**: During a meeting with a customer, the salesperson shares information with them, such as introducing themselves, their company, their products, and services, how their products or services are useful to them, what value add they can provide, and so on. The exchange of information with clients is referred to as information flow. This knowledge will assist the customer in making a purchasing decision. For example, if a client approaches an Education Consultant, the consultant would try to include all relevant information about the college, including its history, context, affiliations, awards, faculty, cost, course structure, and placement of previous batch students.

• **Improved Connection and Understanding**: Communication is essential for establishing a strong connection with your client. A greater understanding is aided by better communication. For example, in the above case, the Education Consultant interacted effectively with the client while exchanging knowledge, resulting in a stronger bond and understanding.

• **Client Coordination and Cooperation**: Improved communication with clients leads to trust and understanding, leading to better client coordination and cooperation. For example, in the above scenario, the Education Coordinator has shared all relevant information with the client, resulting in confidence and understanding. The client will be ready for collaboration and cooperation in the documentation and process execution.

• **Getting People to Consider Change**: Communication aids in understanding the advantages of embracing our bid. This aids in properly training them so that they can gain value if they stick with the move. For example, in the above scenario, the client considers the advantages of being admitted to the college recommended by a consultant.

• **Basis for Action**: If you communicate more effectively with your client, he will be more likely to take action that is beneficial to you. For example, after the Education Consultant has effectively communicated the whole process, the client can take steps to complete the necessary paperwork for college entry.

• **Developing Good Human Relations**: The best way to establish a relationship with a customer is to communicate with them. The sales process is not complete until the customer has purchased your goods or services. You must work to establish a positive relationship with them because, as a customer, they will provide additional business and references. For example, once a client is pleased with the counselor, he enrolled in college, and now he has friends, family, and juniors in high school or college who are seeking his advice about choosing the best college for them.

Communication Principles

We all know that communication is one of the most critical tools in the sales process, and we can use it effectively to get the most out of it. To achieve the best and optimal results, you must learn to communicate effectively and efficiently.

• **Straightforward and Easy to Understand**: The Salesperson follows the idea of consistency by using vocabulary that is both clear and easy to understand. The communicator must deliver the message in its original form, without any information distortion. It should not cause any ambiguity or misinterpretation. If you're dealing with a customer who isn't well-educated, for example, speaking in a technical language with a lot of jargon won't help you. Using local dialects and tones, on the other hand, can improve communication and comprehension.

• **Adequacy and Consistency:** The information or message conveyed to the recipient must be clear, complete, and sufficient in every way. The data must be appropriate and in line with the organization's goals, strategies, processes, and policies. When dealing with a customer, you must have sufficient and reliable product and service details. For example, when buying and selling used vehicles, the dealer performs a thorough inspection and assessment of the vehicle using accurate and up-to-date details.

• **Acceptable Timings:** This concept is extremely useful in customer communication; the Salesperson must learn to use timings correctly. During the conversation, you can look for the best times to pitch your goods and services, as well as the best ways to close sales. For example, you can connect the dots from a casual conversation with a client and compare the same with products and services and provide value to them.

• **Seeking Feedback:** This concept aims to obtain the client's attention by asking whether he has fully understood the communication and whether he has any questions.

• **Get the Client's Attention:** This idea is true, and it helps to get the client's attention by using effective and efficient communication. You ensure that a client is completely attentive and interested in your interaction when speaking with them. To get the client's attention, for example, you can highlight his pain points and how you can fix them from time to time.

The Stages of Sales Communication

Communication takes place in phases, and learning and recognizing these stages will help you communicate with your clients more effectively and gain an advantage. These are the stages:

1.**The Sender**: This is the first phase in the communication process, in which information is communicated verbally or in writing. The Sender's goal is to create a letter, send it to the receiver, and make sure he understands it. The Sender is the Salesperson who initiates contact with the client at this point.

2. **Forming Message or Information:** At this point, the sender drafts the message that will be communicated to the

receiver or client. Developing contents, collecting information, drafting mail or a presentation, and so on are all examples of forming a message.

3. Message or Information Encoding: At this point, the message or information is translated into a simple format to understand, such as symbols, images, graphics, a presentation, audio, or video.

4. Transmission by Channel and Medium Selection: This stage aims to choose the best mode of communication, such as a personal meeting, a virtual meeting, a phone call, or a letter. The Sender must choose the appropriate channel and medium for communication to make it more efficient and powerful. Other considerations to consider include cost, necessity, need, and urgency.

5. Decoding and Understanding: At this stage, the message is obtained at the receiver's end, after which he decodes it and translates it to an understandable format.

6. The Recipient and Reception: The Recipient receives the message, decodes it, and fully comprehends it at this stage. At this point, the recipient is referred to as the Buyer or Client.

7. Response and Feedback: At this point, the response and feedback are collected to determine if the message has been received and understood by all parties and if they are on the same page.

This is a standard step-by-step communication method used in sales. All interactions, whether consciously or unconsciously, obey these stages or steps. Study, practice, and master communication skills. You will become a better communicator who can better communicate with clients, create better relationships, and turn them into business.

CHAPTER 11: SALES LEADERSHIP

The word "sales leadership" is gaining popularity in sales these days. During the sales process, sales leadership entails strategic thinking, decision-making, and encouraging and empowering customers. They will see and leverage opportunities as a Sales Leader, and they look forward to turning each situation into a new opportunity.

"To be conscious of yourself having a wider horizon and taking actions efficiently to build or give value to your clients" is how sales leadership is described.

Another concept of sales leadership is: "Sales leaders are great visionaries, and they represent a bigger picture in the minds of their clients, so they don't just sell, but they build value for their clients." Sales leaders assist their customers in discovering potential possibilities, and they are willing to pay more if they see and appreciate the importance of the opportunity.

We'd appreciate how one of the most valuable skills a salesperson must develop, practice, and specialize in is sales leadership. It will assist you in the sales process and improve your effectiveness and efficiency in sales. It will also assist you in being a Highly Effective Salesperson.

There are four basic characteristics of a sales leader

• **Long-Term Vision:** Sales leaders often have a bigger picture in mind, which they convey through their efforts and interactions with customers. They aren't looking for a quick sale; instead, they want to develop a long-term partnership that will lead to a long-term business relationship.

• **Adaptable to Change:** Sales leaders constantly strive to provide and create value for their customers, so they constantly update themselves, learn new things, collect more knowledge, and continue to explore new avenues for better opportunities and solutions. This enables them to be more adaptable and changeable, resulting in better performance.

• **Beyond Selling:** Sales leaders still see the big picture and realize that their work entails more than just selling. They are willing to go the extra mile to find innovative and improved solutions for their clients to bring value to their lives.

• **Focus on Relationships:** Sales leaders are never satisfied with a single sale to a client; instead, they strive to develop stronger connections and relationships with them, resulting in long-term mutually beneficial relationships in which they provide value and receive repeat business.

Sales Leadership's Purpose and Function

The purpose and function of sales leadership are to generate and expand revenue, which can be accomplished by opening new doors or finding new clients. The following is the aim and role of sales leadership:

• **Concentrate on the Big Picture:** The fundamental aim and role of sales leadership are to keep an eye on the big picture and the result. Sales leaders are regarded as visionaries because they possess powerful ideas and methods for achieving better results. They convert and communicate their vision to their clients, causing them to expand their horizons to see future outcomes that can favor the client and their personal or organizational development.

• **Strategic Thinking:** Sales leaders think all of the time creatively, assessing each situation as an opportunity and planning ahead of time. Sales leaders control their sales battlefield, where they think strategically and make decisions to beat the competition and attract customers. This entails determining the best solution, plan, and pacing to optimize Sales and Revenue.

• **Setting Goals and Objectives:** Setting Goals and Objectives guided by schedules or deadlines is another essential function of Sales Leadership. When a Salesperson takes care of and owns these expectations and priorities, they automatically become more dedicated and work harder to achieve them. These targets and objectives have been renamed SMARTER goals and objectives, and they are as follows:

Specific and Clear: They must be precise and concise.

Measurable: In terms of numbers, income, quantity, or consistency, they must be measurable.

Achievable: They must be Achievable but Difficult to complete.

Time-bound: Time limits must be set on a regular, weekly, monthly, quarterly, or annual basis.

Ethical: The aims and priorities must be ethical, and only ethical methods can be used to accomplish them.

Rewarding: Sufficient incentives should be provided for achieving the goals.

• **Command Instinct:** Sales Leadership skills allow the salesperson to take firm control of the sales process, enhance their status, and give them an advantage when negotiating and persuading clients. This helps them establish a strong personality and rapport with the customer, contributing to confidence and comfort.

• **Change Agent**: Sales Leadership skills allow the salesperson to master the art of change, which is the one thing that is constant in the world. This is due to the unpredictability and uncontrollable changes in the environment, technology, culture, economy, and consumer preferences, among other things. As a result, salespeople are often willing to learn new skills and patterns and unlearn old ones to keep up with evolving business dynamics. It allows them to provide more value to their customers by providing alternative solutions.

• **Sales Intuition**: Sales Leadership skills assist the salesperson in developing the ability to see, observe, and build opportunities, as well as transform each opportunity that comes their way. Their abilities function as a team and are extremely beneficial when working with clients during sales interactions and client meetings.

• **Mutually Beneficial Relationship**: One of the essential goals of sales leadership is to deliver the best outcomes for all. Throughout the sales process, each party has their strategy, opinions, points of view, personality, reaction, and expertise. In such a scenario, the Salesperson's position as Sales Leader becomes critical, as they must strike a balance and bring all stakeholders together. Each stakeholder feels involved, understood, and benefited in some way.

• **Closing Deals & Overcoming Objections**: Sales Leadership skills assist the salesperson in developing Highly Effective Sales Skills, which leads to closing deals and

127

overcoming any client objections. These abilities can be acquired through daily practice and perseverance, and they will still be beneficial in any circumstance.

Sales Leadership Principles

If you want to be a successful salesperson, you must follow the Sales Leadership Principles. You must have a strong set of principles that you demonstrate while preparing, making decisions, solving problems, and other tasks. Salespeople follow these Principles regularly to develop their skills and achieve their goals. The following are the examples of these Principles:

1. Customer-First Approach: This principle focuses on putting the client first, and you will go to great lengths to please and fulfill them. Any business aims to meet the needs of their customers by providing better and enhanced goods and services, resolving their issues, providing alternative solutions, and assisting them in every way possible to attract and retain them.

2. Self-Awareness and Improvement: One of the most valuable qualities of a sales leader is becoming more self-aware and continuously developing their knowledge and skills. This allows them to stay current and informed about emerging developments and opportunities in the industry.

3. Technical and Tactical Proficiency: This Principle focuses on acquiring Technical Proficiency through learning, expertise, and experience and applying them in more sophisticated and effective ways to achieve better results. This philosophy emphasizes lifelong learning and improvement for both the individual and the team.

4. Ownership: This principle emphasizes taking care of and being accountable for the activities and outcomes of the defined objectives, goals, and outcomes. Sales leaders focus on the long term and do not make compromises or sacrifices to achieve short-term goals. They take ownership of the problem and try to find solutions that add value to their customers. This contributes to the creation of an atmosphere that encourages accountability and transparency.

5. Accountable for High Standards: This principle motivates salespeople to perform at the highest level of their skill and performance. It aids in developing good sales and people management practices and creating value for all parties involved.

6. Innovation and Creativity: The Principles of Innovation and Creativity assist the salesperson in developing innovative and creative ideas to make it easier and provide better goods and services to customers.

7. Judgment and Instinct: This Sales Leadership Principle focuses on skills and competence, allowing them to have good Judgmental and Instinctive abilities. This gives them various perspectives on the situation or issue, allowing them to come up with unique solutions.

8. Develop Trust and Respect: This Sales Leadership Principle allows the salesperson to listen carefully, talk candidly, and treat others equally and respectfully. They foster a culture of trust and respect within the organization and receive the same in exchange, which aids in developing better connections and rapport, resulting in better and stronger relationships with all stakeholders.

9. Seek Feedback: They feel that by accepting constructive criticism, they will immediately change. Feedback aids in generating better and fresh ideas, leading to significant improvements in products, facilities, and distribution and packaging methods, among other things.

This principle allows the Salesperson to concentrate on driving and producing great results every time. These outcomes are accurate in terms of quantity, consistency, and timeliness. These outcomes are the product of choosing the best plan, selecting the right main inputs, taking the right approach, and implementing it on time.

The Steps to Becoming a Sales Leader

Sales leaders are the catalysts for long-term success and a transformation in business efficiency and business outcome. Sales leaders strive to improve their competencies with their teams, resulting in improved results at all levels. You will improve Sales Leadership qualities and mentality by following a step-by-step process. These steps can be summarized as follows:

Step 1: Visualize Yourself as a Sales Leader

Developing into a Sales Leader is a gradual process that can be accomplished over time. The first step is to imagine or see yourself as a sales leader. You must complete the following tasks in this step:

Analyze and Understand What You Want: In this phase, you must consider and comprehend why you want to be a Sales Leader and how it will benefit you and others.

Write What You Want: This will assist you in memorizing, focusing, and creating a desire to work toward your target. You'll become more focused on achieving them.

Study Sales Leaders: Study Sales Leaders, paying attention to what you value about them, including how they speak, their tone, vocabulary, behavior, movements, attitudes, motivation, body language, and skills. How they respond in various circumstances and to different types of people.

Improve Yourself: Once you've started watching Sales Leaders, you'll want to start acting like them and seeing how they handle each of their responsibilities. Learn the experience and skills you'll need to succeed as a sales leader.

Step 2: Learn Sales Leader Skills and Qualities

In this step, you can begin studying the skills and qualities a Sales Leader possesses. You can learn them from various places, including books, online and offline training, peer observation, and so on.

Step 3: Create a Long-Term Vision

Excellent sales leaders have a long-term perspective. The vision describes their ambitions and objectives, as well as those of the company. Sales leaders understand what needs to be achieved, how to accomplish them, and who will be responsible for achieving them. They develop their vision after considering all of the significant internal and external factors that may affect their vision and goals.

Step 4: Strategically Think and Act

You must learn to think and behave strategically as a sales leader. Thinking and behaving strategically entails devising a strategy for achieving desired outcomes. In this phase, you must look for all possible opportunities, obstacles, and challenges and then plan and strategize accordingly to achieve your desired outcome or goals.

Step 5: Connect with Stakeholders

You should learn how to communicate effectively with all stakeholders in this step. First, you should be familiar with all key stakeholders, their roles and responsibilities, and how they can help you succeed. Then you must prepare and strategize how to interact with them and add value to them as well as to yourself.

Step 6: Find the Right Mentor

Finding the right mentor and guide is the most critical aspect of the Sales Leadership journey. Having a great mentor and guide will make the journey much easier and quicker. They share their knowledge and best practices, which you can use to improve and apply in your own business to achieve quicker and better results.

Step 7: Monitor Your Progress and Improve

It's important to keep track of your progress and results because only then will you be able to tell whether you're on the right track. Once you've identified your path, you can take necessary or corrective steps if needed to enhance your journey.

This is the step-by-step method for developing Sales Leadership Qualities and Skills or becoming an effective Sales Leader. These measures necessitate a high degree of long-term dedication and practice. This will assist you in gaining faith, trust, and appreciation, as well as assisting you in being a better salesperson and sales leader.

CONCLUSION

Salespeople are subjected to a huge amount of negativity. For any deal they close, they are likely to receive a slew of unanswered calls and emails, not to mention prospects who are uninterested or even aggressive.

It can be challenging to get through all of the "No's" on the way to a "Yes."

Selling isn't an exact science. There is no one-size-fits-all strategy that guarantees success every time. It's an art form that necessitates tact, elegance, sensibility, and perseverance. No matter where you are in your sales career, it is always beneficial to learn how to practice the art of selling.

In this book, you've found all the tools, techniques and advice to create your own strategy. Now it's your turn, put everything you've learned into practice and become a great salesperson.

You're on the right track, good luck!

MOTIVATIONAL SALES QUOTES

- "Our greatest weakness lies in giving up. The most certain way to succeed is always to try just one more time." -*Thomas Edison*
- "Become the person who would attract the results you seek." -*Jim Cathcart*
- "Don't watch the clock; do what it does. Keep going." -*Sam Levenson*
- "Everything you've ever wanted is on the other side of fear." -*George Addair*
- "The secret of getting ahead is getting started." -*Mark Twain*
- "Quality performance starts with a positive attitude." -*Jeffrey Gitomer*
- "Do you want to know who you are? Don't ask. Act! Action will delineate and define you." -*Thomas Jefferson*
- "Setting goals is the first step in turning the invisible into the visible." -*Tony Robbins*
- "A goal is a dream with a deadline." -*Napolean Hill*
- "Don't be afraid to give up the good to go for the great." -*John D. Rockefeller*
- "High expectations are the key to everything." -*Sam Walton*

- "Innovation distinguishes between a leader and a follower." -*Steve Jobs*

UP

URANUS
PUBLISHING

www.ingramcontent.com/pod-product-compliance
Lightning Source LLC
Chambersburg PA
CBHW071659210326
41597CB00017B/2247